ZENLIGHTENMENT

Mind-Opening Insights
About Love, Life, and Happiness

(Revised and expanded 3rd Edition)

partially written,
thoroughly edited and prefaced

by

Michael Pastore

ZORBA PRESS

Ithaca, New York

www.ZorbaPress.com

Zenlightenment — Mind-Opening Insights About Love, Life, and Happiness. (Revised and expanded 3rd edition). Copyright © 2015 by Michael Pastore. All rights reserved. The copyrighted material is this collection as a whole, the Foreword and Preface, and the individual quotations and passages and story written by the authors Michael Pastore (MP), Hokkumeboshi, and Ming Li. Without prior permission from the publisher, this work may not be redistributed, may not be reproduced, and may not be resold.

Published by Zorba Press, July 2015
For more information about this work, see our web site: http://www.zorbapress.com

The three quotations on page 4 are by Hokkumeboshi, Henry David Thoreau, and Marcus Aurelius. The translation of Kazantzakis on pages 13–14 is by Thanasis Maskaleris.

ISBN+10: 0-927379-09-0
ISBN+13: 978-0-927379-09-0

Library of Congress Control Number: 2014903634

Cover Art and Book Design by Ann Warde
Printed and bound in the United States of America.
For sales, permissions, and all other inquiries, please contact Zorba Press by email at books@zorbapress.com

Printings: cv012, ip021
BCDEFGHIJKLMNOPQRSTUVWXYZA
0102030405060708091011121314151617181920

The One Thing

You have a duty to perform.
Do anything else, do any number of things,
occupy your time fully,
and yet,
if you do not do this task,
your time will have been wasted.

— Rumi

This is not a book
it's a bright path calling you
home to your true self.

Whenever a man hears it he is young,
and Nature is in her Spring.

Human Life!
Its duration is momentary,
its substance in perpetual flux,
its senses dim, its physical organism perishable,
its consciousness a vortex,
its destiny dark,
its repute uncertain,
the material element is a rolling stream,
the spiritual element dreams and vapor,
life a war and sojourning in a far country,
fame oblivion.
What can see us through?

The sands of Time
so quickly pass
Through our life's
slender hourglass.

Before the sea foam
washes all away
Be quick to love!
Not tomorrow, love Today.

— Michael Pastore

Contents

The One Thing 3
Human Life 4
The Sands of Time So Quickly Pass 6
Contents 7
Dear Mantis 8

Foreword (to the 3rd Edition, 2015) 9
Preface (to the Original Edition) 13

Action 15
Seeing 25
Freedom 31
Joy 41
Thoughts Made Visible 51
False Paths 61
Nectar, Ambrosia, & Ceiling Gruel 67
Advice to Seekers and Finders 75
Men of Truth 89
Holiness 99
Self Transformation 109
Love 125
Children 137
Sacred Dust 145
Zenlightenment 151

The Wise Woman and the Dying Man 157

Index — Feast of Authors 164

About Zorba Press 172

Dear mantis — Can you show me one moment that is not a miracle?

— *Hokkumeboshi*

Foreword

> All journeys have secret destinations
> of which the traveler is unaware.
>
> — Martin Buber

When I look back at my life over the past seven years, I am amazed at how many times I had forgotten the most essential things, and lost the way.

Headfirst I plunged into pleasant and interesting distractions. Though I stayed on my vegetarian diet of superfoods, I sat in front of a computer more, and I exercised less. Instead of looking at trees and lakes, I hunted meretricious treasures on the Internet. Instead of reading the best books — reading Homer and Kazantzakis, Rumi and Hafez, Goethe and Hesse, Emerson and Melville, and Whitman and Thoreau — I buried my head inside technical manuals, to grasp the arcane workings of software connected with publishing ebooks, audiobooks, and paperbacks. Astonishingly, for anyone who knows me, I stopped taking my early-morning walks into the woods, my long bike-rides in beautiful places, and my inspiring night walks under the stars.

I saw life as a race, and every day an opporunity to travel faster and farther. And yet the whole truth was never far from my heart: every day of our lives can be a marvelous journey. These secret destinations — what our soul cries for — stay with us always in our tears, and in our dreams.

What do we need to change our struggling selves, and to transform our suffering world? ... Our minds thirst for wisdom, and our hearts are ravenous for love.

One source of wisdom is books. And strangely, it is often the older books and authors that can best help us to re-discover the newest and most important themes.

One of these true books is the great novel *Siddartha*, written in 1919 by Hermann Hesse. Siddartha, the book's hero, rebels against the luxurious comforts of his father's house, and then begins a journey to find enlightenment and meaning in his life. After more than seven years of wandering and pondering, he has mastered three basic lessons: how to think, how to wait, and how to fast. One morning, in the city, Siddartha meets Kamala, the most beautiful of courtesans, whose favors can be enjoyed only by the wealthiest men. So Siddartha abandons his spiritual quest and devotes himself to work, business, money-making, and the ecstatic pleasures of the flesh.

Like the mature Siddartha, we — the men and women of the Western world — have forgotten our quest for meaning, integrity, and truth. With jobs, mortgages, and never-ending work to do — and with thousands of ludicrous advertising messages bombarding us every week — few among us have the time, the mind, or the energy to read and to think about ideas that might change our inner and outer lives.

Some years ago — to solve my own problem of how to stay connected to these vital ideas — I collected the quintessence of my readings into a book titled *Zenlightenment*.

The theme of this anthology comprises answers

to what I call "the three essential questions." How can we open our hearts, to live each day with more happiness, more wisdom, and more love? ... How can we train our minds for the deepest concentration and creativity, so that we can solve any problem that confronts us? ... And how can we re-make our precious planet Earth into a place of harmonious living, kindness, and peace?

The best books reveal a common solution: that the answer can be found by cultivating genuine relationships. Genuine relationships with other persons and living beings, with meaningful work, with the creative arts, with books, with the natural world, and with our own true self.

In the deep books, the greatest thinkers have examined their own lives then written from the heart. They call us to renew ourselves, to simplify our lives, to reconnect with our childlike qualities of uniqueness, curiosity, openness, kindness, joy. They urge us to heal ourselves, then after we have become whole, to reach out to other human beings.

If you've ever looked at the world and felt confusion and despair about human violence and stupidity — and wondered how you can make a good life for yourself amidst this chaos — then *Zenlightenment* might lead you to what you need. When you find a quote here that wakes your mind, lightens your heart and makes you sing out loud — say, for example, a gem by Ralph Waldo Emerson — then explore it further in this way: Read a collection of essays by Mr. Emerson, which are free, and easily available on the Internet.

Never lose hope, never lose faith in yourself, faith in the infinite love and courage inside human beings. One day — little by little, and by colossal leaps — this love and courage will transform the entire planet into a community that lives like one great family.

Until we reach that Paradise of sincerity and caring, each of us can live simply and lovingly. Find the work which expresses what is unique inside you. Do not waste your free time: use it for activities that enrich your mind. Stop staring at screens, and instead find ways to care for all the other persons — and other living creatures — who cross your path and enter your daily life.

On the darkest nights we see the brightest stars. Whenever we look up at the starry nights, we see the vast and unimaginable beauty and goodness in our own bright souls.

Seven years ago I wrote and edited *Zenlightenment* to give courage and wisdom to others. I never imagined that I myself would get lost inside life's labyrinth, and once again become a seeker and a wanderer. Fortunately, this book has come home again, to remind its author about life's most essential and wonderful things.

Nevertheless, Dear Reader, this book is still for you, for your amazing journey through the maze of life. It will guide you to secret destinations, to the daring dreams of youth, to hope and compassionate action, and to the perennial mysteries glowing in the heart of love.

Michael Pastore
July 2015
Ithaca, New York

Preface

The passages in this volume have been chosen because they nourish the spirit, illuminate our inner nature, and point the way to a life more resonant with meaning, more alive with joy.

"A wise saying," says the mystic poet Hokkumeboshi, "is a feast for ten thousand men inside one rice grain."

All great literature, by necessity, is a distilled essence of our passions, insights, and experiences. Microcosmic aphorisms are the quintessences: lightning flashes between writer and reader, superconcentrated diamonds of human truth.

In the following passage I attempt to capture the gleam of these diamonds. An impossible task, utter nonsense, sheer folly! Like the finger pointing to the finger pointing to the moon.

The paradise that men ceaselessly seek is not located in some distant place or time. It has nothing to do with science, technology, money, progress, or material prosperity. Because it cannot be seen or touched, no man can give it to another. It is found only within the heart. We can attain this inner paradise only by our own efforts, by our own insights, and by our own deep love.

The remarkable Nikos Kazantzakis has said this with far more passion and tenderness:

> "All things in this world have a hidden meaning, I thought. Humans, animals, trees, stars — they are all hieroglyphics. Woe to the one — and joy, too — who begins to sense them and attempts

to decipher them. The moment you see them, you do not understand them. You think they are really humans, animals, trees, stars, as all appearances. It is only years later, too late, you really come close to fathoming them ... "

This book is a celebration of the kingdoms within us; a treasure map leading to the land of hidden meanings, unheard melodies, secret joys. Too many men lead their outward lives as if these sacred things do not exist. Others, like myself, know that they exist but cannot easily find them and keep them. Years and years we spend, desperately looking for love and happiness.

Of course, we come at last to realize that happiness and love can never be found by looking. Only by seeing with the heart, and by giving love.

Begin today, begin right now! It is never too late to open yourself, to change yourself, to free yourself. My friend Hokkumeboshi, every time we meet, hugs me like a child, then laughs as he whispers into my ear —

> The door is always
> open. Why do you keep on
> searching for the key?

Michael Pastore

ACTION

Man is so made that
whenever anything fires his soul,
impossibilities vanish.

— *La Fontaine*

Pray to God,
but keep rowing to the shore.

— Russian saying

Our main business is not to see
what lies dimly in the distance,
but to do what lies clearly at hand.

— Thomas Carlyle

People are always blaming their circumstances for what they are. I don't believe in circumstances. The people who get on in this world are the people who up and look for the circumstances they want, and if they don't find them, make them.

— George Bernard Shaw

When you fix your heart on one point,
then nothing is impossible for you.

— Buddha

What would life be if we had no courage
to attempt anything?

— Vincent van Gogh

It is not because things are difficult
that we do not dare;
it is because we do not dare
that they are difficult.

— Seneca

If you start to take Vienna, take Vienna.

— Napoleon Bonaparte

The faster we flee from our Destiny,
the harder she throws us
back to the place where we need to begin.

— Ming Li

He that riseth late must trot all day.

— Benjamin Franklin

It is better to follow the Voice
inside and be at war with the whole
world, than to follow the ways of
the world and be at war with
your deepest self.

— Michael Pastore

When one must, one can.

— Yiddish saying

He who has a firm will molds the world to himself.

— Johann Wolfgang von Goethe

For the most part, all the external
side of life must be neglected; one
should not bother about it.
Do your own work.

— Leo Tolstoy

Little by little grow the bananas.

— African saying

The great end of life is not knowledge, but action.

— T. H. Huxley

The path of others
is full of danger; your own
path tastes like honey.

— Hokkumeboshi

Everything is possible. A man is never lost.
Whatever he may have done, there's always some
moment in his life when he has a chance of
retrieving himself and becoming a good and useful
member of the community.

— Papillon

If a man has a WHY to live
he can conquer any how.

— Friedrich Nietzsche

The only meaningful way of life
is activity in the world;
not activity in general but
the activity of giving and caring for fellow creatures.

— Erich Fromm

If you can't help your friend with money,
at least help him with a sympathetic groan.

— Yiddish saying

If I did not work,
these worlds would perish.

— *Bhagavad Gita*

Roast pigeons do not fly into your mouth.

— Yiddish saying

Two Travelers

A saunter of a hundred yards,
was pondered by a rat,
He found a blister on his paw —
and that was the end of that.
A journey of ten thousand miles,
a lion swore to dare,
A hunter's arrows pierced his heart! —
yet nightfall found him there.

— Michael Pastore

Fate is a monkey
who will treat you the same way
you treat other men.

— Hokkumeboshi

Do somethin' that means somethin'.

— John Steinbeck,
in *The Grapes of Wrath*

The philosophers have only interpreted the world in various ways; the point is to change it.

— Karl Marx

Man, we have not yet reached the end of our struggles: a risky, noble, and glorious task awaits us, and we must face it without delay.

— Homer

However many words you read,
however many you speak,
what good will they do you if
you do not act upon them?

— *The Dhammapada, The Path of Wisdom*

Never despair. There are always actions — some small and some enormous — that you can do to renew your life, and to improve the lives of others. A good life is an active life, when your actions are inspired by love, by passion, and by compassion.

— Michael Pastore

If I had six hours to chop wood,
I would spend the first five hours
sharpening my axe.

— Abraham Lincoln

... for it is only when a man goes out into the world with the thought that there are heroisms all round him, and with the desire all alive in his heart to follow any which may come within sight of him, that he breaks away as I did from the life he knows, and ventures forth into the wonderful mystic twilight land where lie the great adventures and the great rewards.

— Arthur Conan Doyle

We are very near to greatness:
one step and we are safe:
can we not take the leap?

— Ralph Waldo Emerson

So far a journey! ...
From the bottom of my heart
to my fingertips.

— Hokkumeboshi

SEEING

As I sat on the back of the Drop or God's pond ... I said to my companion I declare this world is so beautiful
that I can hardly believe it exists.

— *Ralph Waldo Emerson*

I believe a leaf of grass
is no less than the journey-work
of the stars.

— Walt Whitman

Some persons can see
a mosquito's eye,
while to others
even a mountain is invisible.

— T'ang Meng-lai

The foregoing generation beheld God and nature face to face; we, though their eyes. Why should we not also enjoy an original relation to the universe? Why should we not have a poetry and philosophy of insight and not of tradition, and a religion by revelation to us, and not the history of theirs?

— Ralph Waldo Emerson

The eye through which you see God
is the same eye
through which God sees you.

— Meister Eckhart

A fool sees not the same tree that a wise man sees.

— William Blake

The greatest thing a human soul ever does in the worldis to SEE something, and tell what it SAW in a plain way. Hundreds of people can talk for one who can think,but thousands can think for one who can see. To see clearly is poetry, prophecy and religion all in one.

— John Ruskin

By learning what he sees,
a person becomes a pundit.

— Tamil saying

Talent is the capacity
to direct intense concentration
on the subject ...
A gift of seeing
what others have not seen.

— Leo Tolstoy

In order to have original, uncommon, and perhaps even immortal thoughts, it is enough to estrange oneself so fully from the world of things for a few moments, that the most ordinary objects, and events appear quite new and unfamiliar. In this way their true nature is disclosed.

— Arthur Schopenhauer

One minute of illumination
is worth a thousand years of know nothing.

— Joyce Cary

When a man gets this feeling of 'reality', he knows that nothing in the world could be so important as keeping it. He tries every possible method of reminding himself not to forget, not to stop fighting to achieve it. What is more, in this state of intensity, it becomes clear that it can be achieved. He sees now as something that is self-evident that he possesses a true will, the ability to focus clearly on an objective and then to achieve it in the most economical way. But then he descends back to his lower storey, and can only remember dimly that he had a vision. The sleep comes back.

— Colin Wilson

What truly is within
is manifested without.

— Chinese saying

I refer, of course, to the Romantic Movement, which was more than a change of style: it was a sudden expansion of consciousness — an expansion into realms of sensibility not previously accessible to the human imagination.... Our duty at the moment, as creative writers and its critics, is to maintain the impetus of that revolution.

— Herbert Read

The teeth are smiling,
but is the heart?

— African saying

To see a World in a Grain of Sand
And a Heaven in a Wild Flower
Hold Infinity in the palm of your hand
And Eternity in an hour.

— William Blake

Knowledge does not come to us in details,
but in flashes of light from heaven.

— Henry David Thoreau

Freedom

Place your head inside a lion's jaws, then tickle him beneath the chin.

— *Hokkumeboshi*

Man is free the moment he wishes to be.

— Voltaire

The real slavery of Israel in Egypt
was that they had learned to endure it.

— Hasidic saying

A slave is he who cannot speak his thought.

— Euripides

If a man speaks or acts
with a pure thought,
happiness follows him like a shadow
that never leaves him.

— Dhammapada

A sycophant advised Diogenes:
"If you would only learn to flatter King Alexander,
then you would not have to eat lentils."
Diogenes replied:
"If you would only learn to eat lentils,
then you would not have to flatter Alexander."

— Plutarch

He is always a slave who cannot live on little.

— Horace

It is better to die of hunger, but in a state of
freedom from grief and fear,
than to live in plenty, but troubled in mind.

— Epictetus

The task of tyrants of the future
will be to make people love their servitude.

— Aldous Huxley

When a messenger suggested that the Spartans surrenderto King Xerxes, a Spartan general replied:
"You do not know what you are advising us to do, for you know what it is to be a slave, but the sweetness of freedom you have never tasted.

If you felt it, you would tell us to fight for it, not with spears only, but with axes."

— Plutarch

There can be no freedom without responsibility.

— Socrates

For the tragedy of our lives is not created entirely from within. "Character," says Novalis, in one of his questionable aphorisms, "character is destiny." But not the whole of our destiny. Hamlet, Prince of Denmark, was speculative and irresolute, and we have a great tragedy in consequence. But if his father had lived to a good old age, and his uncle had died an early death, we can conceive Hamlet's having married Ophelia, and got through life with a reputation of sanity, notwithstanding many soliloquies, and some moody sarcasms toward the fair daughter of Polonius, to say nothing of the frankest incivility of his father-in-law.

— George Eliot

When the mouse laughs at the cat, there is a hole nearby.

— Nigerian saying

What is it to be free? ...
I say it is to say what you think,
to do what you feel.

— Greek sailor (told to M.P.)

Freedom is not a cake that drops into one's mouth
and is there for the swallowing,
but a citadel to be stormed with the saber.
Whoever receives freedom from foreign hands
remains a slave.

— Nikos Kazantzakis

Look your Tiger in the eyes
and he is half tamed.

— Ming Li

If I am not free, I cannot sing;
and if I cannot sing, I die.

— Somerset Maugham

There are two kinds of slaves:
slaves who will die to win their freedom,
and slaves who sing praises to their chains.

— Ming Li

I am freed at last from thoughts
that made me grieve,
As though a sword had cut
a rope from my neck,
And limbs grow light
when the heart sheds its care:
Suddenly I seem to be
flying up to the sky!

— Po Chu-I

Socialism, reduced to its simplest legal and practical expression, means the complete disregarding of the institution of private property by transforming it into public property, and the division of the resultant public income equally and indiscriminately among the entire population. Thus is reverses the policy of Capitalism, which means establishing private property or "real" property to the utmost physically possible extent, and then leaving distribution of income to take care of itself. The change involves a complete moral volte-face. In Socialism private property is an anathema, and equal distribution of income the first consideration. In capitalism private property is cardinal, and distribution left to ensue from the play of free contact and selfish interest on that basis, no matter what anomalies it may present.

— George Bernard Shaw

> Is there no life but these alone —
> Madman or slave must man be one?
>
> — Matthew Arnold

And so fell George's last hope; — nothing before him but a life of toil and drudgery, rendered more bitter by every little smarting vexation and indignity which tyrannical ingenuity could devise.

— Harriet Beecher Stowe

> Free, dost thou call thyself?
> Thy ruling thought I would hear of,
> and not that thou hast escaped from a yoke.
>
> — Friedrich Nietzsche

"Mr. Heathcliff," said I, "this is the talk of a madman, and your wife, most likely, is convinced you are mad; and, for that reason, she has borne with you hitherto; but now that you say she may go, she'll doubtless avail herself of the permission. You are not so bewitched, ma'am, are you, as to remain with him of your own accord?"

— Emily Brontë

Personal history repeats itself until this great moment: the moment we take action to transform the depths of our inner selves.

— Michael Pastore

My storehouse
Burnt down
Nothing obscures the view
Of the bright moon.

— Masahide

A surging, seething, murmuring crowd of beings that are human only in name, for to the eye and ear they seem naught but savage creatures, animated by vile passions and by the lust of vengeance and of hate. The hour, some little time before sunset, and the place, the West Barricade, at the very spot where, a decade later, a proud tyrant raised an undying monument to the nation's glory and his own vanity.

During the greater part of the day the guillotine had been kept busy at its ghastly work: all that France had boasted of in the past centuries, of ancient names, and blue blood, had paid toll to her desire for liberty and for fraternity. The carnage had only ceased at this late hour of the day because there were other more interesting sights for the people to witness, a little while before the final closing of the barricades for the night.

— Emma Orczy

This Task

Start a huge,
foolish project like Noah.
It makes absolutely no difference
what people think of you.

— Rumi

There is but an inch of difference
between the cushioned chamber
and the padded cell.

— G. K. Chesterton

... I began to be very well contented with the life I led, if it might have but been secured from the dread of the savages.

But it was otherwise directed: and it may not be amiss for all people who shall meet with my story, to make this just observation from it, viz. How frequently, in the course of our lives, the evil which in itself we seek most to shun, and which when we are fallen into it is the most dreadful to us, is oftentimes the very means or door of our deliverance, by which alone we can be raised again from the affliction we are fallen into. I could give many examples of this in the course of my unaccountable life; but in nothing was it more particularly remarkable, than in the circumstances of my last years of solitary residence in this island.

— Daniel Defoe

Every stroke of my brush
is the overflow
of my inmost heart.

— Sengai Gibon

ALPINE GLOW

Our lives are Swiss, —
  So still, so cool,
  Till, some odd afternoon,
The Alps neglect their curtains,
  And we look farther on.

Italy stands the other side,
  While, like a guard between,
The solemn Alps,
The siren Alps,
  Forever intervene!

— Emily Dickinson

JOY

Surely joy is the condition of life.

— *Henry David Thoreau*

The highest wisdom is continual cheerfulness.
Such a state, like the region above the moon,
is always clear and serene.

— Michel de Montaigne

Bird sounds generally are seldom describable. We
have no symbols to represent such sounds on paper,
hence we are as powerless to convey to another the
impression they make on us as we are to describe
the odours of flowers.

— William Henry Hudson

Hey! dogs rolling in
the dirt! Stop having more fun
than Umeboshi!

— Hokkumeboshi

Children think not of what is past,
nor what is to come,
but enjoy the present time,
which few of us do.

— Jean de La Bruyere

Very little is needed to make a happy life. It is all
within yourself, within your way of thinking.

— Marcus Aurelius

There is only one way to happiness,
and that is to cease worrying about things which are
beyond the power of our will.

— Epictetus

My dearest Princess
lies trapp'd in the darkest cave,
Guarded by seven
tigers who never
sleep. Her name: Happiness. Slay
fear to set her free.

— Hokkumeboshi

Rapture and ecstasy can only be discovered by
practicing what the ancients called Mindfulness.
We must learn how to surrender,
how to give complete attention,
how to lose our selves in the profound mystery
of this moment here and now.

— Michael Pastore

In spite of everything, rejoice.

— Hasidic saying

Do not lose the spirit of reverence,
no matter how wicked are the
people with whom you come in contact;
nor the habit of peaceful joy
when great misfortunes come.

— Kaibara Ekken

I'm not the pheasant plucker,
I'm the pheasant plucker's son,
And I'm only plucking pheasants
Till the pheasant plucker comes.

— English tongue twister

Growth in wisdom may be exactly measured
by decrease in bitterness.

— Friedrich Nietzsche

> Quit seeking wisdom!
> Look into the eyes of men
> who give and give love.
>
> — Hokkumeboshi

> The moment I embrace Love,
> she gives me her daughters to sleep with —
> Wisdom and Joy.
>
> — Ming Li

Their whole life was ordered not by law, stature or rule, but according to their free will and pleasure. They arose when they pleased. They ate, drank, worked and slept when the spirit moved them. No one awoke them, forced food or drink upon them or made them do anything else. Gargantua's plan called for perfect liberty. The only rule of the house was:

DO WHAT THOU WILT

because men that are free, of gentle birth, well-bred and at home in civilized company, possess a natural instinct that inclines them to virtue and saves them from vice. This instinct they name their honor. Sometimes they may be depressed or enslaved by subjection or constraint; for we all long for forbidden fruit and covet what is denied us. But they usually apply the fine forces that tend to virtue in such a way as to shake off the yoke of servitude.

— Francois Rabelais

If you do not drive in sleet through the woods
singing, you have to drive through crying.

— Czech saying

Man will hereafter be called to account
for depriving himself of the good things
which the world lawfully allows.

— Talmud

Enjoy the world gently, enjoy the world
gently; if the world is spoiled, no one
can repair it, enjoy the world gently.

— Nigerian song

Why do we love looking at the stars?
Is it because the infinity above
mirrors the vast beauty
of the universe within us?

— Ming Li

If the day and night are such
that you greet them with joy,
and Life emits a fragrance like flowers
and sweet-scented herbs,
is more elastic, more starry,
more immortal —
that is your success.

— Henry David Thoreau

I wandered till I found
the meaning of my life:
sacred moments;
persons who I love;
dreams to make alive.

— Michael Pastore

Beauty
is just the right amounts
in just the right places.

— O. Thoreau, in *Thoreau Bound:
A Utopian Romance in the Isles of Greece.*

I've never spoken like this to any one else before, and I don't suppose I ever shall again. Here is Nature, man, the greatest force on earth, the mother, the mistress, benificent, wonderful! You are a creature of cities. Stay with me here for a day or two, and the joy of all these things will steal into your blood. You, too, will know what peace is.

— E. Phillips Oppenheim

At a small distance from the house my predecessor had made a seat, overshaded by an hedge of hawthorn and honeysuckle. Here, when the weather was fine, and our labour soon finished, we usually sat together, to enjoy an extensive landscape, in the calm of the evening. Here too we drank tea, which now was become an occasional banquet; and as we had it but seldom, it diffused a new joy, the preparations for it being made with no small share of bustle and ceremony. On these occasions, our two little ones always read for us, and they were regularly served after we had done. Sometimes, to give a variety to our amusements, the girls sung to the guitar; and while they thus formed a little concert, my wife and I would stroll down the sloping field, that was embellished with blue bells and centaury, talk of our children with rapture, and enjoy the breeze that wafted both health and harmony.

In this manner we began to find that every situation in life might bring its own peculiar pleasures: every morning waked us to a repetition of toil; but the evening repaid it with vacant hilarity.

— Oliver Goldsmith

"Truly," quoth he, "the dear world is as fair here as in the woodland shades. Who calls it a vale of tears? Methinks it is but the darkness in our minds that bringeth gloom to the world."

— Howard Pyle, *Robin Hood*

Hail to thee, blithe Spirit!
Bird thou never wert,
That from Heaven, or near it,
Pourest thy full heart
In profuse strains of unpremeditated art.

— Percy Bysshe Shelley, *To a Skylark*

The superior man is always satisfied,
the mean man is always full of distress.

— Confucius

Who would wish to banish the diagnostic writers, as Plato banished the poets from his republic? But should they be accorded the dominant place which they have assumed in our day? — should they be permitted to eclipse the curative writers? I suggest that we need above all at present those who can restore for us a feeling for the true aims of living, who can remind us of the goodness in men, bring back the joy of life and give one a sense of human hope.

— Van Wyck Brooks

O how I laugh when I think of my vague indefinite
riches. No run on my bank can drain it,
for wealth is not possession but enjoyment.

— Henry David Thoreau

What smells like lilacs?
Not roses, not marigolds,
not cherry blossoms.

— Hokkumeboshi

Thoughts
MADE
VISIBLE

Art is the earthen vessel that carries divine fire from man to man.

— *Hokkumeboshi*

Who shall describe what befell him then?
What poet has the persuasiveness to reconcile
the length of the days he now lived
with the brevity of life?
What art is vast enough to evoke simultaneously
his slight, cloaked figure and the whole high
spaciousness of his gigantic nights?

— Rainer Marie Rilke

Art is not for its own sake, but as a means of
communicating with humanity.

— Modest Petrovich Mussorgsky

Each man's soul sleeps for a hundred years,
dreaming it shall one day be awakened
by a kiss of Truth.

— Ming Li

The writer who dives deeply enough
into the streams of his own heart
soon discovers he is swimming
in the same sea that encompasses all humankind.

— Michael Pastore

Art begins when a man wishes to immortalize
the most vivid moment
he has ever lived.

— Arthur Symons

The thoughts you think will irradiate you
as if you are a transparent vase.

— Maurice Maeterlinck

There is no more Heraculean task than to think
a thought about this life and then get it expressed.

— Henry David Thoreau

Everything has been thought of before,
but the problem is to think of it again.

— Johann Wolfgang von Goethe

I write poetry
the foolish days I forget
I am the poem.

— Hokkumeboshi

Whenever I read a marvelous book
I am changed into a child
hiding behind a peach tree,
eavesdropping
on the conversation of wise men.

— Ming Li

The man who writes about himself and his own time is the only man who writes about all people and all time.

— George Bernard Shaw

Nature is beautiful, simple and direct — for in her, nothing is lacking and nothing is superfluous.

— Leonardo da Vinci

These novels will give way, by and by, to diaries or autobiographies — captivating books, if only a man knew how to choose among what he calls his experiences that which is really his experience, and how to record truth truly!

— Ralph Waldo Emerson

The way to write well is to live intensely.

— Virginia Woolf

To forget is the same thing as to throw away.

— African saying

The solution to the artist's overwhelming problem is to be found only in untiring and unremitting LABOR. In this way, the technical matters will be thoroughly mastered, so that the artist is free for the great struggle to imbue the work with vitality, and the essence of his inner life. If Paganini, who expressed his whole soul through the strings of his violin, spent three days without practicing, he lost what he called the rapport with his instrument, meaning the sympathy between the wooden frame, the strings, the bow, and himself. If he had lost this alliance, he would have been no more than an ordinary player on the street.

> CONSTANT WORK IS THE LAW OF ART,
> AS IT IS THE LAW OF LIFE,

for art is idealized creation. Therefore, the great artists and sublime poets never wait for commissions or for buyers. They are ceaselessly creating — today, tomorrow, always. The result is the habit of work, and the profound understanding of the work's difficulties, which keep them in close connection with the Muse and her creative powers. Canova lived in his studio, as Voltaire lived in his study; and so must Homer and Phidias have lived.

> [And Begin Working Now ...]

"Then, I hope you mean to work, my dear treasure," said Hortense.
"Yes, of course," said the artist. "I will begin tomorrow."
"Tomorrow is our ruin!" said his smiling wife.

— Honore de Balzac

When you point your finger at the moon,
a fool will look at your finger.

— Chinese saying

Think like a philosopher,
speak like a common man.

— Aristotle

The world is a comedy to those who think,
a tragedy to those who feel.

— Horace Walpole

My method is to take the utmost trouble to find the right thing to say, then say it with the utmost levity.

— George Bernard Shaw

Always tell the truth in the form of a joke.

— Armenian saying

I spent five days writing one page, last week ...
By July or August I hope to begin the denouement.
What a struggle it will have been, my God! What
a struggle! What back-breaking work, what
discouragements!

— Gustave Flaubert

Genius is eternal patience.

— Michelangelo

Heaven and earth have sworn
the Truth shall be disclosed.

— Yiddish saying

Poets understand
how to coax ten elephants
into one small bag.

— Hokkumeboshi

The painted picture of a dumpling
does not take one's hunger away.

— Master Kyogen

Stranger, you have poor judgment and a faulty memory. Poor judgment, because whenever something is forbidden, it is inevitable that people should be tempted to do that thing. Faulty memory, because you have already forgotten what I told you.

— Denis Diderot

God grant me the power to finish the story as I have begun it. I have never done anything better; everything else is still and lifeless compared to it.

— E.T.A. Hoffmann (about *The Golden Flower Pot*)

My favorite piece of music is the one
we hear all the time, if we are quiet.

— John Cage

How many a man has dated a new era in his life
from the reading of a book! The book exists for
us, perchance, which will explain our miracles
and reveal new ones. The at present unutterable
things we may find somewhere uttered. These same
questions that disturb and puzzle and confound us
have in their turn occurred to all the wise men; not
one has been omitted; and each has answered them,
according to his ability, by his words and his life.

— Henry David Thoreau, from *Walden*

Reading is that fertile miracle of communication
effected in solitude.

— Marcel Proust

God made man because he loves stories.

— Yiddish saying

"Vigorous writing is concise" is six syllables too
long. Be brief.

— Michael Pastore

A person who can write a long letter with ease,
cannot write ill.

— Jane Austen

> But James Joyce bores me stiff — too terribly
> would-be and done-on-purpose,
> utterly without spontaneity or real life.
>
> — D. H. Lawrence

Happiness usually makes people good, and Niels strove earnestly to make their lives so beautiful, noble, and useful that there should never be any pause in the growth of their souls toward the human ideal in which they both believed. But he no longer thought of carrying the standard of his ideal out into the world; he was content to follow it. Once in a while, he would take out some of his old attempts, and then he would always wonder if it was really he who had written these pretty, artistic tilings. His own verses invariably brought tears to his eyes, but he would not for anything in the world have changed places with the poor fellow who wrote them.

— Jens Peter Jacobsen (*Niels Lyhne*)

The superior man abides in his room. If his words are well spoken, he meets with assent at a distance of more than a thousand miles. How much more then from near by! If the superior man abides in his room and his words are not well spoken, he meets with contradiction at a distance of more than a thousand miles. How much more then from near by. Words go forth from one's own person and exert their influence on men.

— I Ching

Writing, when properly managed, (as you may be sure I think mine is) is but a different name for conversation: As no one, who knows what he is about in good company, would venture to talk all; -- so no author, who understands the just boundaries of decorum and good breeding, would presume to think all: The truest respect which you can pay to the reader's understanding, is to halve this matter amicably, and leave him something to imagine, in his turn, as well as yourself.

— Laurence Sterne

A wise man, Agathon, compacts his words,
And many thoughts compresses into few.

— Aristophanes

I think it better that in times like these
A poet keep his mouth shut, for in truth
We have no gift to set a statesman right;
He has had enough of meddling who can please
A young girl in the indolence of her youth,
Or an old man upon a winter's night.

— William Butler Yeats
(*On Being Asked For A War Poem*)

If ever a writer of novels or poems runs out of ideas, instead of weeping and tearing out his hair, he should bow his head humbly and give thanks to his all-wise Muses. For then he would be forced to rely on one astonishing technique: "Tell the whole truth."

— Michael Pastore

False Paths

Ev'rywhere men weep
suffer, search for the lost hat
sitting on their head.

— *Hokkumeboshi*

To drink a deadly poison is better than worry.

— Solomon Ibn Gabirol

Trusting to escape scrutiny, by fixing the public gaze upon the exceeding brightness of military glory — that attractive rainbow, that rises in showers of blood — that serpent's eye, that charms to destroy — he [President James Polk] plunged into war.

— Abraham Lincoln

I think that there is nothing, not even crime, more opposed to poetry, to philosophy, ay, to life itself, than this incessant business.

— Henry David Thoreau

Are you not ashamed of heaping up the greatest amount of money and honor and reputation, and caring so little about wisdom and truth and the greatest improvement of the soul, which you never regard or heed at all?

— Socrates

Destructiveness is the outcome of unlived lives.

— Erich Fromm

Blind man with blind dog:
I cannot prevent you from
eating yellow snow.

— Hokkumeboshi

The cost of a thing is the amount of what I call life
which is required to be exchanged for it,
immediately or in the long run.

— Henry David Thoreau

Lost man! He who has
no great love to go to is
easily seduced.

— Michael Pastore

Worry about your own soul
and the next person's body —
not the opposite.

— Hasidic saying

If you try to cleanse others, like soap,
you waste away in the process.

— African saying

An ungrateful son is like a wart on his father's face.

— Chinese saying

The tragedy of a man is what dies inside himself
while he still lives.

— Albert Schweitzer

When each day ceases
to be play and ecstasy,
we philosophize.

— Hokkumeboshi

It is better to light one small candle
than to curse the darkness.

— Chinese proverb

Neither a man nor a nation can survive
without a sublime idea.

— Fyodor Dostoyevsky

One does not get crucified, one crucifies oneself.

— Bulgarian saying

Ancient tribes believed that the moment a man
tells a lie, the lie becomes a voracious lizard. First
the creature devours the man's own heart, then he
consumes the hearts of everyone he loves.

— Ming Li

The future of civilization depends on our
overcoming the meaninglessness and hopelessness
which characterizes the thought of men today.

— Albert Schweitzer

Aurea rumpunt tecta quietem [Latin].
Golden palaces break (or disturb) one's rest.

— Seneca

Technology is a stunning woman: first she turns your head, then she twists it off at the neck.

— O. Thoreau
(*Thoreau Bound —
A Utopian Romance in the Isles of Greece*)

The concern for man and his destiny must always be the chief interest of all mechanical efforts.

— Albert Einstein

The better life! Possibly, it would hardly look so, now; it is enough if it looked so then. The greatest obstacle to being heroic is the doubt whether one may not be going to prove oneself a fool; the truest heroism is, to resist the doubt; and the profoundest wisdom, to know when it ought to be resisted, and when to be obeyed.
— Nathaniel Hawthorne

O God! O God! We have been an exile in another land and a stranger in our own.

— Thomas Wolfe

Haste, haste if thou wouldst fail.

— Thales

Nectar Ambrosia & Ceiling Gruel

I'm not an ordinary man,
and I'm not going to live
an ordinary life.

— *Theodore Dreiser*

Tasty ceiling gruel!
Clear as a lake I drink this
bowl of shining stars.

— Hokkumeboshi

Of all forms of caution, caution in love is perhaps the most fatal to true happiness.

— Bertrand Russell

I have never seen a man whose love of virtue equaled his love of woman.

— Confucius

When I look back at the past and think how much time has been wasted in vain, how much time was lost in delusions, in errors, in idleness, in ignorance of how to live, how I did not value time, how often I sinned against my heart and spirit my heart bleeds. Life is a gift, Life is happiness, each minute might have been an age of happiness. If youth only knew!

Now, changing my life, I am being reborn into a new form. Brother! I swear to you that I shall not lose hope and shall preserve my spirit and heart in purity. I shall be reborn to a better thing. That is my whole hope, my whole comfort.

— Fyodor Dostoyevsky

It is no shame to ask, and no calamity to be refused.

— Russian saying

You never touch
This soft skin
Surging with hot blood.
Are you not bored,
Expounding the Way?

— Yosano Akiko

A man can make more
trouble for himself than one
hundred enemies.

— Hokkumeboshi

He who binds to himself a joy
Does the winged life destroy;
But he who kisses the joy as it flies
Lives in eternity's sun rise.

— William Blake

If a fool be associated with a wise man even all his
life, he will perceive the truth as little as
a spoon perceives the taste of soup.

— Dhammapada

Adventures are to the adventurous.

— Benjamin Disraeli

Woodcutters come with
saws and axes, rabid to
chop down my bonsai.

— Hokkumeboshi

The inhabitants of Pa resemble wild apes;
Fierce and lusty, they fill the mountains and prairies.
Among such as these I cannot hope for friends
And am pleased with anyone who is even remotely human.

— Po Chu-I

If you are patient in one moment of anger,
you will escape a hundred days of sorrow.

— Chinese proverb

To be nobody-but-yourself in a world which is doing its best, night and day, to make you everybody else — means to fight the hardest battle which any human being can fight; and never stop fighting.

— e.e. cummings

Two-thirds of help is to give courage.

— Irish saying

The cobra will bite you
whether you call him
cobra or Mr. Cobra.

— Indian proverb

There are gods who dwell in the Sacred Mountains, watching the world, helpless to help us, laughing with wild laughter, weeping with inconsolable tears. Now and then, between divine dalliances and ambrosial feasts, they drop down to Earth, guised in mortal countenance and garb. Here they attempt to teach us the unteachable: to enjoy life; to face obstacles with fearless audacity; to respect all living things.

— Ming Li

An angry fist cannot strike a smiling face.

— Chinese saying

He had enough energy for three lifetimes.

— Maxim Gorky, writing about Tolstoy

The fool and water will go the way they are diverted.

— African saying

Watching the dishes
pile up in the sink ... Ah! My
unfulfilled desires!

— Hokkumeboshi

If you do not change your direction
you are likely to end up
where you are headed.

— Chinese saying

Faith is the bird that sings
while the dawn is still dark.

— Rabindranath Tagore

And should it be granted to me to live one
hundred and ten years, I hope that a vital and true
comprehension of nature may radiate from every
one of my lines and dots.

— Hokusai

An early morning walk
is a blessing for the whole day.

— Henry David Thoreau

If each new day, as our human life unfolds itself like the pages of an illuminated fairy-book, is not a caravanserai of marvels, a ship of treasures, an island of enchantment, with its own sun and moon and high particular stars, what, in heaven's name, is the value of being alive at all?

— John Cowper Powys

If you can walk, you can dance.
If you can talk, you can sing.

— Zimbabwe Proverb

Nothing matters save
the first moment my teeth bite
into this sweet plum.

— Hokkumeboshi

It is no enough that we do our best, sometimes we have to do our duty.

— Winston Churchill

'Tis true little Kay is at the Snow Queen's, and finds everything there quite to his taste; and he thinks it the very best place in the world; but the reason of that is, he has a splinter of glass in his eye, and in his heart. These must be got out first; otherwise he will never go back to mankind, and the Snow Queen will retain her power over him.

— Hans Christian Andersen

Their Delight In Learning. ...
The people in general are easy-going, cheerful, clever, and fond of leisure. When they must, they can stand heavy labor, but otherwise they are not very fond of it. In intellectual pursuits, they are tireless. When they heard from us about the literature and learning of the Greeks (for we thought there was nothing in Latin except the historians and poets that they would enjoy) it was wonderful to behold how eagerly they sought to be instructed in Greek.

— Thomas More

Charming women
know the secret of the spider:
Spin your web and wait.

— Hokkumeboshi

Coffee should be dark as night, hot as hell,
sweet as love.

— Turkish saying

Did you not know that people
hide their love,
Like the flower that seems
too lovely to be picked?

— Wu-ti

Advice to Seekers and Finders

Do not depend on others. There is no grace, no help to be had from the outside.

— *Buddha*

The extraordinary is never found
along the ordinary path.

— Johann Wolfgang von Goethe

When Fate throws a knife at you
there are two ways to catch it —
by the handle, or by the blade.

— Chinese saying

It was my constant rule in life never to avoid the
conversation of any man who seemed to desire it; for
if good, I might profit by his instruction; if bad, he
might be assisted by mine.

— Oliver Goldsmith

You have invented a very useful younger brother
called Ernest, in order that you may be able to come
up to town as often as you like. I have invented an
invaluable permanent invalid called Bunbury, in
order that I may be able to go down into the country
whenever I choose. Bunbury is perfectly invaluable.

— Oscar Wilde

The virtues of society are the vices of the saint.

— Ralph Waldo Emerson

Life is not a problem to be solved,
but a reality to be experienced.

— Soren Kierkegaard

Nothing great is ever achieved
without enthusiasm.

— Ralph Waldo Emerson

Never put off until tomorrow
what you can do the day after tomorrow.

— Mark Twain

Men will always be mad,
and those who think they can cure them
are the maddest of all.

— Voltaire

Whoever fights a monster should see to it that in the process he does not become a monster.

— Friedrich Nietzsche

"Heyday!" quoth he. "What's that you are saying? the labour-saving machines? Yes, they were made to "save labor" (or, to speak more plainly, the lives of men) on the piece of work in order that it might be expended — I will say wasted — on another, probably useless, piece of work. Friend, all their devices for cheapening labor simply resulted in increasing the burden of labour."

— William Morris

Nothing in human affairs is worth any great anxiety.

— Plato

A broad margin of leisure is as beautiful in a man's life as it is in a book ... What are three score years and ten hurriedly and coarsely lived, to moments of divine leisure in which your life is coincident with the life of the universe?

We live too fast and too coarsely, just as we eat too fast, and do not know the true savor or our food.

— Henry David Thoreau

Trust men and they will be true to you;
treat them greatly and they will show themselves great.

— Ralph Waldo Emerson

When we talk about evil persons this may give rise to evil thoughts, and hence, God forbid, to bringing evil into the world. Therefore, let us talk only about the good ways of righteous men, and so bring good into the world.

— Hasidic saying

When a man follows his own Way
He becomes one with himself.
Standing still, he travels far.
Without moving, he moves men.
Needing nothing, his goal rushes to meet him.
Fearing nothing, he is free.
Serene within, he loves others selflessly.
Because he laughs at your self-made suffering,
his love heals you and makes you whole.

— Ming Li

The soul is healed by being with children.

— Fyodor Dostoyevsky

Laughing turns witches
into sandwiches; dragons
into dragonflies.

— Hokkumeboshi

The ideal man bears the accidents of life
with dignity and grace,
making the best of circumstances.

— Aristotle

Nothing deters a good man
from doing what is honorable.

— Seneca

As a solid rock is not shaken by the wind,
wise people falter not amidst praise and blame.

— Dhammapada

It is by believing in roses that we bring them to bloom.

— Anatole France

All the grandeur in the world is not equal in value
to a good friend.

— Voltaire

The lure of the distant and difficult is deceptive. The great opportunity is where you are.

— John Burroughs

There is nothing noble in being superior to some other men. The true nobility is in being superior to your previous self.

— Hindu saying

To be awake is to be alive ... We must learn to reawaken and keep ourselves awake, not by mechanical aids, but by an infinite expectation of the dawn ...

— Henry David Thoreau

Defy and resist every thing that hurts your body; Accept and embrace every thing that hurts your soul.

— Ming Li

Peace is not an absence of war, it is a virtue, a state of mind, a disposition for benevolence, confidence, justice.

— Spinoza

If you bow at all, bow low.

— Chinese saying

The Difference

Such different men! The Saint and con —
Those who pray, and those who prey upon.
Say cons: the gap is great and tall —
But Saints believe the difference small.

— Michael Pastore

Man is not the creature of circumstances.
Circumstances are the creatures of men.

— Benjamin Disraeli

Who troubles himself about his ornaments or fluency is lost. This is what you shall do: Love the earth and the sun and the animals, despise riches, give alms to every one that asks, stand up for the stupid and the crazy, devote your income and labor to others, hate tyrants, argue not concerning God, have patience and indulgence toward the people, take off your hat to nothing known or unknown or to any man or number of men, go freely with powerful uneducated persons and with the young and with mothers of families, read these leaves in the open air every season of every year of your life, re-examine all you have been told at school or church or in any book, dismiss whatever insults your own soul, and your very flesh shall have the richest fluency not only in its words but in the silent lines of its lips and face and between the lashes of your eyes and in every motion and joint of your body.

— Walt Whitman

Genius is a long patience.

— Georges Louis Leclerc de Buffon

If we cease to believe that we will become gods,
we will become worms.

— Henry Miller

I have never bothered or asked in what way I was useful to society as a whole; I contented myself with expressing what I recognized as good and true. That has certainly been useful in a wide circle; but that was not the aim; it was the necessary result.

— Johann Wolfgang von Goethe

Greatness is the poise of laughter and
lightheartedness,
while running like hell to grab your sacred goal.

— Michael Pastore

What wise man can flourish in the crevice
between the folly of the world,
that tells men to desire money,
and the nonsense of the books,
that tell a man to desire nothing at all?

— Ming Li

Renew thyself, completely each day.
Do it again, and again, and forever again.

— Zengzi, quote in Thoreau's *Walden*

Feel kindly toward everyone,
but be intimate only with the virtuous.

— Confucius

Each dawn I follow
my heart, not stopping till I
hear the nightingale.

— Hokkumeboshi

Paint a picture of your Paradise and walk in.

— Nikos Kazantzakis

Hide your good deeds
and keep your functioning a secret.
Look like a simpleton or fool.

— Master Sozan

The professor stared. "Have you," he said, "really spent your time in studying such nonsense?"

— Mary Shelley

This is by no means the least of life's rules:
To let things alone.

— Baltasar Gracian

The mother with a broad sweep of her arms cried out: "Listen for the sake of Christ! You were old dear people, you are all good people. Open up your hearts. Look around without fear, without terror. Our children are going off into the world. Our children are going, our blood is going for the truth; with honesty in their hearts they open the gates of the new road — a straight, wide road for all. For all of you, for the sake of your young ones, they have devoted themselves to the sacred cause. They seek the sun of new days that shall always be bright. They want another life, the life of truth and justice, of goodness for all."
— Maxim Gorky

Have Ithaka always in your mind;
to arrive there is what you are destined for.
But do not in the least hurry the journey.
Better that it lasts for years,
and you are old when you reach the island
rich with what you have gained on the way
not expecting Ithaka to give you wealth.

— C.P. Cavafy, *Ithaka*
(translation by Thanasis Maskaleris)

Si quieres que otro se ria
cuenta tus penas, Maria.
(If you want to make someone laugh,
tell him your troubles, Maria.)

— Spanish proverb

[Alexandr to his Uncle:]
I shook my head, and told him that I did not want to talk to him of my work but of what was nearer to my heart. Then I began to tell him of my love, of my sufferings, of the emptiness of my heart. I began to be carried away and thought that the story of my sufferings was breaking through the crust of ice, that his eyes were not quite unbedewed by tears, when suddenly he burst out laughing! I looked at him, he had a handkerchief in his hands; he had been trying to control himself all the time I was talking, at last he could hold out no longer. I stopped in dismay.

— Ivan Goncharov, *A Common Story*

"Now don't be stupid over this. I don't require you to fall in love with my boy, but I do think you might try and understand him. You are nearer his age, and if you let yourself go I am sure you are sensible. You might help me. He has known so few women, and you have the time. You stop here several weeks, I suppose? But let yourself go. You are inclined to get muddled, if I may judge from last night. Let yourself go. Pull out from the depths those thoughts that you do not understand, and spread them out in the sunlight and know the meaning of them. By understanding George you may learn to understand yourself. It will be good for both of you."

To this extraordinary speech Lucy found no answer.

— E. M. Forster, *A Room With A View*

I should like to remind you that apart from what has already been said on this subject, the nature of wit is such that its bite must be like that of a sheep rather than a dog, for if it were to bite the listener like a dog, it would no longer be wit but abuse.

— Giovanni Boccaccio

To the lonely house in the pine wood people sometimes came for advice on subjects too recondite for even those extremes of elucidation, the parish priest and the tavern. These people were always well received, and their perplexities were attended to instantly, for the Philosophers liked being wise and they were not ashamed to put their learning to the proof, nor were they, as so many wise people are, fearful lest they should become poor or less respected by giving away their knowledge. These were favourite maxims with them:

You must be fit to give before you can be fit to receive.

Knowledge becomes lumber in a week, therefore, get rid of it.

The box must be emptied before it can be refilled. Refilling is progress.

A sword, a spade, and a thought should never be allowed to rust.

— James Stephens

Improvise! Learn to improvise! Whenever the great plan breaks, pick up the ball then run with all your power to the light.

— Michael Pastore

> No great man ever complains of
> want of opportunity.
>
> — Ralph Waldo Emerson

DESIROUS of embracing the whole circle of human knowledge, and anxious to bequeath to the world a concrete symbol of his encyclopedic genius and a display in keeping with his pecuniary resources, Baron Alexandre d'Esparvieu had formed a library of three hundred and sixty thousand volumes, both printed and in manuscript ...

— Anatole France

> "Tell me where's your lovely maiden,
> Whom you sang of erst so well,
> As a flame that through your bosom
> Pierced with rare, enchanted spell."
>
> "Ah, that flame is long extinguished!
> And my heart is cold above.
> And this little book the urn is
> For the ashes of my love."
>
> — Heinrich Heine

> Be calm, stoical, impassive.
> Do not show anger.
> Smile at misfortune.
> If you sprain your ankle, laugh.
>
> — Ian Fleming

We think too much, and we feel too little.

— Charlie Chaplin

Thinking tomorrow's
hunger, yesterday's chickens —
I drop today's egg.

— Hokkumeboshi

Self-Restraint When Angered

When the surging tide of wrath has broken
the floodgates of thy breast, refrain
thy tongue, so words in passion spoken
do not reveal you to be foolish, mad, and vain.

— Sappho (fragment 27)

The chains of habit are too weak to be felt
until they are too strong to be broken.

— Samuel Johnson

The greatest discovery of my generation
is that a human being can alter his life
by altering his attitudes.

— William James

MEN OF TRUTH

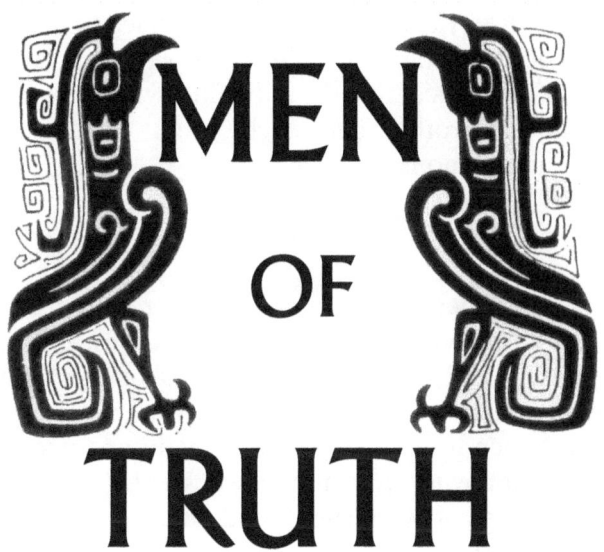

First and last
what is demanded of genius
is love of truth.

— *Johann Wolfgang von Goethe*

What is tolerance? It is the consequence of humanity. We are all formed of frailty and error; let us pardon reciprocally each other's folly - that is the first law of nature. ... It is clear that the individual who persecutes a man, his brother, because he is not of the same opinion, is a monster.

— Voltaire

There are times when example is better than precept for stirring or for soothing human passions; and so I propose to follow up the words of consolation I gave you in person with a history of my own misfortunes, hoping thereby to give you comfort in absence. In comparison with my trials you will see that your own are nothing, or were slight, and you will find your troubles easier to bear.

— Peter Abelard

Invisible energy springs
from the spirit of illuminated men.
Those who attain perfect stillness
vibrate at the highest speeds.

— Ming Li

What a piece of work is a man! how noble in reason!
how infinite in faculty! in form and moving how
express and admirable! in action how like an angel!
in apprehension how like a god!

— William Shakespeare

"That's marvelous," said the Lord Mayor. "But what is your plan?"
"The most good for the largest number of needy — a universal pledge of activism based upon such luminaries in the avant garde of solitude as Jeremy Bentham, John Stuart Mill, Albert Schweitzer, Percy Shelley, Leonardo da Vinci, Nikos Kazantzakis, and the theory of hotspots."

— Michael Charles Tobias,
The Adventures of Mr Marigold

I am not an Athenian or a Greek,
but a citizen of the world.

— Socrates

When Socrates was asked,
"Why do we never see in you any sign of fear?"
he answered,
"Because, unlike yourselves,
if I lost any of my possessions I would not grieve."

— Xenophon, *Memorabilia*

They live in the moment, fully,
and the radiance which emanates from them
is a perpetual song of joy.

— Henry Miller

I have learnt through bitter experience the one
supreme lesson to conserve my anger,
and as heat conserved is transmuted into energy,
even so our anger controlled can be transmuted
into a power which can move the world.

— Gandhi

Except ye be converted and become as little
children, ye shall not enter into the kingdom of
heaven.

— Jesus of Nazareth

A great man is he who has not
lost the heart of a child.

— Mencius

Now I shall go down and lead my people
from darkness into light, from suffering to
happiness, and from Evil to Good!

— Zoroaster

Those who want the fewest things
are nearest to the gods.

— Socrates

To understand others is to have knowledge;
To understand oneself is to be illumined.
To conquer others needs strength;
To conquer oneself is harder still.
To be content with what one has is to be rich.

— Lao Tzu

What can it serve to reveal to the world what I have gained in these painful strivings? The Truth is not easily learned by those filled with lust and hatred. It is something which costs trouble, full of mystery, profound, and hidden from the coarser spirit: he whose mind is veiled in darkness by earthly desires is unable to see it.

— Buddha

Mine is a life full of joy in the midst of incessant work. In not wanting to think of what tomorrow will bring for me I feel as free as a bird ...

— Gandhi

I am going to be a storm — a burning flame —
I need to make a war against whole armies;
I have ten hearts; I have one hundred arms;
I feel too strong to fight against mere humans —
(He shouts as loudly as he can shout.)
Bring me giants!

— Edmund Rostand, *Cyrano de Bergerac*

If it were not laughed at, it would not be Tao.

— Lao Tzu

The superior man goes through his life without any preconceived course of action or any taboo. He merely decides for the moment what is the right thing to do.

— Confucius

It was his opinion that the land was dying for want of trees. He added that, having no very pressing business of his own, he had resolved to remedy this state of affairs.

— Jean Giono, *The Man Who Planted Trees*

Be bold! Be free! Be truthful!

— Brenda Ueland

If a state is following the Path, it is a disgrace to be in
Poverty and a low estate therein; if not,
it is a disgrace to be rich and honored therein.

— Confucius

I had power in my hands! And then I felt the irresistible vocation within me! The prisoned millions lay all over the country, deep in the bowels of the earth, calling aloud to me! They shrieked to me to free them! But no one else heard their cry — I alone had ears for it.

— Henrik Ibsen

Bide in silence,
and the radiance of the spirit
will come in and make its home.

— Lao Tzu

Suppose a man is so unhappy as to be born a saint, with keen perceptions, but with the conscience and love of an angel, and he is to get his living in the world; he finds himself excluded from all lucrative works; he has no farm, and he cannot get one; for, to earn money enough to buy one, requires a sort of concentration toward money, which is the selling himself for a number of years, and to him the present hour is as sacred and inviolable as any future hour.

— Ralph Waldo Emerson (*Man the Reformer*, 1841)

The superior man thinks of virtue;
the small man thinks of comfort.

— Confucius

I have nothing new to teach the world.
Truth and non-violence are as old as the hills.

— Gandhi

No, never has a writer [Voltaire] had in his lifetime such influence. Despite exile, imprisonment, and the suppression of almost every one of his books by the minions of church and state, he forged fiercely a path for his truth, until at last kings, popes and emperors catered to him, thrones trembled before him, and half the world listened to catch his every word.

— Will Durant, *The Story of Philosophy*

I am still learning.

— Michelangelo (Motto that he placed over the door of his workshop when he reached the age of 70)

In a week or so, I go to New York, to bury myself in a third-story room, and work and slave on my "Whale" while it is driving through the press. That is the only way I can finish it now,—I am so pulled hither and thither by circumstances. The calm, the coolness, the silent grass-growing mood in which a man ought always to compose,—that, I fear, can seldom be mine. Dollars damn me; and the malicious Devil is forever grinning in upon me, holding the door ajar. My dear Sir, a presentiment is on me,—I shall at last be worn out and perish, like an old nutmeg-grater, grated to pieces by the constant attrition of the wood, that is, the nutmeg. What I feel most moved to write, that is banned,—it will not pay. Yet, altogether, write the other way I cannot. So the product is a final hash, and all my books are botches. I'm rather sore, perhaps, in this letter; but see my hand!—four blisters on this palm, made by hoes and hammers within the last few days. It is a rainy morning; so I am indoors, and all work suspended.

— Herman Melville (letter to Hawthorne)

Don't take my joking too seriously. The feeling I have for you does not make me unjust to other women. I have never had such true sympathy for them as I have now since I cease to look at them with lover's eyes. The tremendous effort they have been making during the last thirty years to escape from the degrading and unwholesome semi domesticity, to which our stupid male egoism condemned them to their and our unhappiness, seems to me to be one of the most splendid facts of our time.

— Romain Rolland

Let us confess it: the human situation is always desperate; and man's life is by nature precarious and mutable, delicately poised in an unstable equilibrium that a little excess of heat or a little shortage of water may completely overthrow. But today, all the normal mischances of living have been multiplied, a million-fold, by the potentialities for destruction, for an unthinking act of collective suicide, which man's very triumphs in science and invention have brought about. In this situation the artist has a special task and duty: the task of reminding men of the depth of their humanity and the promise of their creativity.

— Lewis Mumford

> To enjoy the things we ought,
> and hate the things we ought,
> has the greatest bearing
> on the excellence of character.
>
> — Aristotle

Holiness

Life means for us constantly
to transform into light and flame
all that we are or meet with.

— *Friedrich Nietzsche*

A great man appears
to remind us that we are
goddesses and gods.

— Hokkumeboshi

Silence
is a bridge
between the ear of man
and
the voice of gods.

— Ming Li

However muddy the water is,
the lotus retains its purity;
indeed, it blooms beautifully
just because it grows in the mud.

— Sengai

A man without truthfulness!
I know not how that can be.

— Confucius

Truth is God.

— Gandhi

To be calm, to be serene! There is the calmness of the lake when there is not a breath of wind; there is the calmness of a stagnant ditch. So it is with us. Sometimes we are clarified and calmed healthily, as we never were before in our lives, not by an opiate, but by some unconscious obedience to the all-just laws, so that we become like a still lake of purest crystal, and without an effort our depths are revealed to ourselves. All the world goes by and is reflected in our deeps. Such clarity! obtained by such pure means! by simply living, by honesty of purpose. We live and rejoice. I awoke into a music which no one about me heard. Whom shall I thank for it? The luxury of wisdom! the luxury of virtue! Are there any intemperate in these things? I feel my Maker blessing me. To the sane man the world is a musical instrument. The very touch affords exquisite pleasure.

— Henry David Thoreau (Journal, June 22, 1851)

The goddesses and muses whisper to us
in the rosy-fingered hours of the early morning,
then they knock off for the rest of the day.

— Michael Pastore

God could not be everywhere
so he made mothers.

— Yiddish saying

Nothing can live well except in a
manner that is suited to the way the
sacred Power of the World lives and moves.

— Black Elk

Throw your gods away!
Be sincere in all actions,
loving to all men.

— Hokkumeboshi

> Smiling, always smiling,
> the Master answered — What is Holiness?
> "When you love this moment, this man,
> this morning, this deed before you
> with such a great fire of joy
> the gods within you are set free."

— Ming Li

You say that there is only one way to worship and serve the Great Spirit. If there is only one religion, why do you white people differ so much about it? Why don't you all agree, since you can all read the book? ... We do not understand these things. We are told that your religion was given to your forefathers and has been handed down, father to son. We, also, have a religion which was given to our forefathers and has been handed down to us, their children. We worship in that way. It teaches us to be grateful for all the favors we receive, to love one another, and to be united. We never quarrel about religion because it is a matter which concerns each man and the Great Spirit. We know that the Great Spirit is pleased that we follow the traditions of our forefathers, for in doing so we receive his blessing. He has given us abundance, and strength and vigor for the hunt. When we are hungry, the forest is filled with game; when we are thirsty, we drink at his pure streams; when we are tired, the leaves are our bed. We go to sleep content, and we wake up with gratitude to the Great Spirit. With renewed strength in our limbs, and bounding joy in our hearts, we feel blessed.

— Chief Red Jacket (Sa-Go-Ye-Wat-Ha)

He invited them to look at the sky
and lift their faces to the stars.
(Caelum videre iussit,
et erectos ad sidera tollere vultus.)

— Ovid

Behold this and always love it! It is very sacred, and
you must treat it as such.

— Black Elk

Those who say, do not know;
Those who know, say everything
With the light in their eyes.

— Ming Li

For every thing that lives is holy.

— William Blake

Grace, or the Tao, surrounds us always. It is the light and it is God Himself. Whenever we are open for a moment it enters into us, into every child, into every wise man.

— Hermann Hesse

All do not pray to
the same God, but the same God
hears all our prayers.

— Ming Li

All things are full of gods.

— Thales

God has no religion.

— Mahatma Gandhi

When the heart weeps for what it has lost,
the soul laughs for what it has found.

— Sufi saying

We live happily indeed,
not hating those who hate us!
among men who hate us
we dwell free from hatred!
We live happily indeed,
free from greed among the greedy!
among men who are greedy,
let us dwell free from greed!

We live happily indeed,
though we call nothing our own!
We shall be like the bright gods,
feeding on happiness!

— Buddha

I always think that the best way to know God
is to love many things.

— Vincent Van Gogh

As long as Man continues to be the ruthless destroyer of lower living beings, he will never know health or peace. For as long as men massacre animals, they will kill each other. Indeed, he who sows the seed of murder and pain cannot reap joy and love.

— Pythagoras of Samos

> I hear a sudden cry of pain!
> There is a rabbit in a snare;
> Now I hear the cry again,
> But I cannot tell from where.
>
> But I cannot tell from where.
> He is calling out for aid!
> Crying on the frightened air,
> Making everything afraid!
>
> Making everything afraid!
> Wrinkling up his little face!
> As he cries again for aid;
> — And I cannot find the place!
>
> And I cannot find the place
> Where his paw is in the snare!
> Little One! Oh, Little One!
> I am searching everywhere!

— James Stephens (*The Snare*)

To the poet, to the philosopher, to the saint and sage — all things are friendly and sacred; all events profitable; all days holy; all men divine.

— Ralph Waldo Emerson

Beloved Pan, and ye other gods who haunt this place, give me beauty in the inward soul; and may the outer and the inner man be one.

— Prayer of Socrates

With all your science can you tell me how it is, and whence it is, that light comes into the soul?

— Henry David Thoreau

Self

Transformation

My cup overflows
but you cannot drink from it.
Go to the river.

— *Hokkumeboshi*

Cease striving,
then there will be self-transformation.

— Lao Tzu

Man is afraid of things
that cannot harm him, and he knows it,
and he craves things that cannot be of
help to him, and he knows it; but in
truth the one thing man is afraid of is
within himself, and the one thing he
craves is within himself.

— Martin Buber

If the soul within us does not change,
the world outside us will never change.

— Nikos Kazantzakis

The greatest thing in the world
is for a man to know how to be himself.

— Michel de Montaigne

Your appearance, voice, behavior, and
even your criticism should distribute deep
gratitude and thankfulness to all those
who are in your presence. All your
words should be expressive of a deep
gratitude, like the singing of birds and
insects or the poems of Tagore.

— Georges Ohsawa

Inside Umeboshi
is another Umeboshi
wiser than a god.

— Hokkumeboshi

Afoot and light-hearted I take to the open road,
Healthy, free, the world before me,
The long brown path before me leading wherever I choose.
Henceforth I ask not good-fortune,
I myself am good fortune,
Henceforth I whimper no more, postpone no more, need nothing,
Done with indoor complaints,
libraries, querulous criticisms,
Strong and content I travel the open road.

— Walt Whitman

How the soul of man is changed according
to the light, the climate, the solitude, or
the company it keeps!

— Nikos Kazantzakis

Here, on this seat, may my body dry up,
may my skin and flesh waste away if I
raise my body from this seat until I have
attained the knowledge it is hard to
attain during numerous kalpas.

— Buddha

The world is like the curly tail of a dog:
who can straighten it out?

— Hindu saying

So much of our distress comes from the habit of
regarding life as an enemy, and feeling it our duty to
fight it, instead of seeing it as a friend, loving it and
agreeing with it.

— E. Graham Howe

Waiting for luck is like waiting for death.

— Japanese saying

The more a person knows,
the more luck he will have.

— Burmese saying

Each man is in his Spectre's power
Until the arrival of the hour
When his humanity awake
And cast his Spectre into the Lake.

— William Blake

A man's own self is his friend,
a man's own self is his foe.

— *Bhagavad Gita*

In silence I sit
before sunrises, praying
I will be sincere.

— Hokkumeboshi

Before healing others, heal thyself.

— African saying

Do not think your truth
can be found by anyone else.

— Andre Gide

Let a man strive to purify his thought.
What a man thinks, that is what he is;
this is the eternal mystery.
Dwelling within his Self with thoughts serene,
he will obtain imperishable happiness.
Man becomes whatever he thinks.

— *Upanishads*

What is the call of conscience?
Be what thou art!

— Friedrich Nietzsche

The sharp edge of a razor is difficult to pass over;
thus the wise say the path to salvation is hard.

— *Upanishads*

You cannot travel on the path before
you have become the Path itself.

— Buddha

Be open; desire nothing;
accept everything that comes.
First get the way within right,
then everything in the outside world
will become right.

— Ming Li

Character is destiny.

— Heraclitus

The mind is its own place, and in itself can make
a heaven of hell, a hell of heaven.

— John Milton

Though we travel the world over in search of beauty,
we must carry it within ourselves,
or we shall find it not.

— Ralph Waldo Emerson

Calm the mind,
and the whole world becomes peaceful;
Quiet the heart,
and the whole world is a song of joy.

— Ming Li

Ah, where would be any food for spirituality
without night and the stars?

— Walt Whitman

From my point of view,
it is immoral for a being not to make the most
intensive effort every instant of his life.

— José Ortega y Gasset

The future enters into us,
in order to transform itself in us,
long before it happens.

— Rainer Maria Rilke

Nothing can bring you peace but yourself.
Nothing can bring you peace but the triumph of
principles.

— Ralph Waldo Emerson

There are three things about the superior man that I have not been able to obtain. The true man has no worries; the wise man has no perplexities; and the brave man has no fear.

— Confucius

What comes is not to be avoided, what goes is not to be followed.

— Daibi of Unkan

Zen is doing completely and wholeheartedly whatever you are doing.

— R.H. Blyth

How I had dreamed of college! The inspired companionship of teachers who are friends! The high places above the earth, where minds are fired by minds. And what's this place I've come to? Was the college only a factory, and the teachers machines turning out lectures by the hour on wooden dummies, incapable of response? Was there no time for the flash from eye to eye, from heart to heart? Was that vanishing spark of light that flies away quicker than it came unless it is given life at the moment by the kindling breath of another mind — was that to be shoved aside with, "I'm too busy. I have no time for recitations outside of class hours"?

— Anzia Yezierska

> But often, in the world's most crowded streets,
> But often, in the din of strife,
> There rises an unspeakable desire
> After the knowledge of our buried life.

— Matthew Arnold

If you want to obtain a certain thing, you must first be a certain man. Once you have become a certain man obtaining that certain thing will not be a concern of yours anymore.
— Zen saying

Tityros had in fact become another man. A transformation in his deepest self began the day after he murdered his frivolous bullying brother-in-law. He now understood the whole secret of being a man. Being a man did not consist in possessing a great strong body. One must have ubreakable will-power in one's soul! A horsefly with determination could defeat an ox. Being a man was in the soul, not in the body. The moment he had grasped this idea, Tityros began to change. Gradually his body, too, began getting stronger.

— Nikos Kazantzakis (*Freedom or Death*)

Stubborness is a power ... As for Jonathan the tailor, I assume that from his childhood he craved for learning, and the power of will is strong. There is a saying, 'Your will can make you a genius.' When you are idle, a year is nothing, but if you study day and night with diligence, you sop it up like a sponge.

— I. B. Singer (*Passions*)

When you laugh, laugh like hell. And when you get angry, get good and angry. Try to be alive. You will be dead soon enough.
— William Saroyan

Giant social organisms, like the giant animal species of early times, they be destined to disappear suddenly when they have attained their extreme expansion.

Even if that should be so, even if there should be a solution of continuity in the course of civilization, even then, as again Jules de Galutier also held, we need not despair, for life is a fountain of everlasting exhilaration. No creature on the earth has so tortured himself as Man, and none has raised a more exultant Alleluia. It would still be possible to erect places of refuge, cloisters wherein life would yet be full of joy for men and women determined by their vocation to care only for beauty and knowledge, and so to hand on to a future race the living torch of civilisation. When we read Palladius, when we read Rabelais, we realize how vast a field lies open for human activity between the Thebaid on one side and Thelema on the other. Out of such ashes a new world might well arise. Sunset is the promise of dawn.
— Havelock Ellis

He had succeeded in making her talk, and while she rattled on, he strove to follow her, marvelling at all the knowledge that was stowed away in that pretty head of hers, and drinking in the pale beauty of her face. Follow her he did, though bothered by unfamiliar words that fell glibly from her lips and by critical phrases and thought-processes that were foreign to his mind, but that nevertheless stimulated his mind and set it tingling. Here was intellectual life, he thought, and here was beauty, warm and wonderful as he had never dreamed it could be. He forgot himself and stared at her with hungry eyes. Here was something to live for, to win to, to fight for–ay, and die for. The books were true. There were such women in the world. She was one of them. She lent wings to his imagination, and great, luminous canvases spread themselves before him whereon loomed vague, gigantic figures of love and romance, and of heroic deeds for woman's sake–for a pale woman, a flower of gold. And through the swaying, palpitant vision, as through a fairy mirage, he stared at the real woman, sitting there and talking of literature and art. He listened as well, but he stared, unconscious of the fixity of his gaze or of the fact that all that was essentially masculine in his nature was shining in his eyes. But she, who knew little of the world of men, being a woman, was keenly aware of his burning eyes. She had never had men look at her in such fashion, and it embarrassed her. She stumbled and halted in her utterance. The thread of argument slipped from her. He frightened her, and at the same time it was strangely pleasant to be so looked upon. Her training warned her of peril and of wrong, subtle, mysterious, luring; while her instincts rang clarion-voiced through her being, impelling her to hurdle caste and place and gain to this traveller from another world, to this uncouth young fellow with lacerated hands and a line of raw red caused by the unaccustomed linen at his throat, who, all too evidently, was soiled and tainted by ungracious existence.

— Jack London (in *Martin Eden*)

Ten Tips To Transform Time

1. Life is now. *E sempre l'ora* (Italian) = The right time is always now. Concentrate intensely, wholeheartedly, on whatever you are doing right now.

2. Life is here. The delusion that "life is more exciting somewhere else" is the source of oceans of wasted time.

3. Each day is a new life. (Aurelius). Make a plan in the morning and resolve to let nothing distract you from the plan. Early mornings are for caring for your health, and for creating from the heart. There are never excuses for missing these nourishing and essential things.

4. "Work" is everything you do for a future goal, not for the joy of doing it. Compartmentalize all "work" between your hours of least alertness.

5. Save time by keeping organized. Organize your major systems and projects: Does everything have a plan, a time, and a place? … For each task, ask how it can done most efficiently. Abraham Lincoln wrote: "If I had 6 hours to chop wood, I'd spend the first four hours sharpening my axe."

6. Trust in the wisdom of the Universe. But every night, back up your essential files.

7. Instead of eating out, cook a healthy meal. Instead of inviting people for dinner, invite them for tea.

8. Listen to your heart, then do what gives you joy.

9. Health is the key to everything. With good health, every day of your life can be unique and interesting.

10. Remember to live. Remember to love.

— Michael Pastore

The Spirit stood among the graves, and pointed down to One. He advanced towards it trembling. The Phantom was exactly as it had been, but he dreaded that he saw new meaning in its solemn shape.

"Before I draw nearer to that stone to which you point," said Scrooge, "answer me one question. Are these the shadows of the things that Will be, or are they shadows of things that May be, only?"

Still the Ghost pointed downward to the grave by which it stood.

"Men's courses will foreshadow certain ends, to which, if persevered in, they must lead," said Scrooge. "But if the courses be departed from, the ends will change. Say it is thus with what you show me!"

The Spirit was immovable as ever.

Scrooge crept towards it, trembling as he went; and following the finger, read upon the stone of the neglected grave his own name, EBENEZER SCROOGE.

"Am I that man who lay upon the bed?" he cried, upon his knees.

The finger pointed from the grave to him, and back again.

"No, Spirit! Oh no, no!"

The finger still was there.

"Spirit!" he cried, tight clutching at its robe, "hear me! I am not the man I was. I will not be the man I must have been but for this intercourse. Why show me this, if I am past all hope!"

For the first time the hand appeared to shake.

"Good Spirit," he pursued, as down upon the ground he fell before it: "Your nature intercedes for me, and pities me. Assure me that I yet may change these shadows you have shown me, by an altered life!"

— Charles Dickens (*A Christmas Carol*)

All journeys have secret destinations
of which the traveler is unaware.

— Martin Buber

Yes: I am a dreamer. For a dreamer is one who can only find his way by moonlight, and his punishment is that he sees the dawn before the rest of the world.

— Oscar Wilde

Magical desert!
Kiss the hot sand — it becomes
a cool joyous stream.

— Hokkumeboshi

The Buddha can only tell you the way;
it is for you to make the effort.

— Buddha

Butterly sleeping
peacefully on temple bell —
the bronze gong rings!

— Yosa Buson

Love

What do you seek so
pensive and silent?
What do you need
camerado?
Dear son do you
think it is love?

— *Walt Whitman*

Are Your Lips Soft As A Rose?

Are your lips soft as a rose?
Are your kisses wild and free?
Is your soul as dull as prose —
or
Passionate as poetry?

Is your heart sharp as a thorn?
Will it prick my swelling pride
When you meet my friendliness with scorn
or
Laugh out loud at how I tried?

Thoughts about you — far too bold
Come to me just when they please
How tragic these cannot be told!
Only
whispered to the evening breeze.

There is more beauty in your eyes
Than all the stars in clear night skies.
Let me be the one, and only one
who knows —
Are your lips soft as a rose?

— Michael Pastore, *Sappho At The Edge Of Love*

Madame, tonight at two o'clock I must come to your room; I have something to tell you.

— Stendhal

Love yields in one moment
what years of effort can hardly attain.

— Johann Wolfgang von Goethe

I found the girl dancing the fandango with me so voluptuously that she could not have promised me everything more eloquently in words. What a dance! It burns, it inflames, it carries away. Nevertheless, people tried to assure me that the majority of Spanish men and women who dance it mean no harm by it. I pretended to believe them.

— Giacomo Casanova

Like a snowfall, a woman's love
covers the whole world
and makes it beautiful.

— Ming Li

What is hell? I maintain it is the suffering
caused by the inability to love.

— Fyodor Dostoyevsky

Children of the future Age
Reading this indignant page,
Know that in a former time,
Love! sweet Love! was thought a crime.

— William Blake

Her life was a life of pleasures and homage received. The atmosphere she breathed was love — love her light and her lantern, her daily food. She also had loved, often — very often — but that fire never lasted long enough to make the chains which hold for life. "I wait for him, for the hurricane!" she used to say about love. "Up to now he has never climbed over the walls or swum moats. He has been tame, with no wildness in his eye or madness in his heart. I am waiting for the strong man who will take me out of myself. I want to feel love so strong inside me that I will have to quiver in front of him; now I only know the kind of love my intelligence laughs at."

— Selma Lagerlöf

> Let a man overcome anger by love,
> let him overcome evil by good,
> let him overcome the greedy by liberality,
> the liar by truth.
>
> — Buddha

Ownest, in the times that I have been speaking of, I used to think that I could imagine all passions, all feelings, all states of the heart and mind; but how little did I know what it is to be mingled with another's being! Thou only hast taught me that I have a heart — thou only hast thrown a deep light downward, and upward, into my soul. Thou only hast revealed to me myself; for without thy aid, my best knowledge of myself would have been merely to know my own shadow — to watch it flickering on the wall, and mistake its fantasies for my own real actions. Indeed, we are but shadows — we are not endowed with real life, and all that seems most real about us is but the thinnest substance of a dream — till the heart is touched.

That touch creates us — then we begin to be — thereby we are beings of reality, and inheritors of eternity.

— John Jay Chapman, letter to his wife, which she called: "La miraculosa littera d'amore" — The miraculous love letter.

The truth must be spoken lovingly.

— Henry David Thoreau

He who wishes to be benevolent will not be rich.

— Mencius

While writing a novel as an occupation and distraction for my mind, I conceived the idea of portraying an exclusive and undying love, before, during, and after marriage. Thus I drew the hero of my book proclaiming, at the age of eighty, his fidelity to the one woman he had ever loved.

The ideal of love is assuredly eternal fidelity. Moral and religious laws have aimed at consecrating this ideal. Material facts obscure it. Civil laws are so framed as to make it impossible or illusory. Here, however, is not the place to prove this. Nor has Mauprat been burdened with a proof of the theory; only, the sentiment by which I was specially penetrated at the time of writing it is embodied in the words of Mauprat towards the end of the book: "She was the only woman I loved in all my life; none other ever won a glance from me, or knew the pressure of my hand."

— George Sand

The toughest fiber must melt in the fire of love.
If the fiber does not melt,
it is only because the fire is not strong enough.

— Mahatma Gandhi

To those who are good to me I am good; and
to those who are not good to me I am good.
And thus all get to be good.

— Lao Tzu

I have always heard it said that to do a kindness to
clowns is like throwing water into the sea.

— Cervantes

Regardless of our color, race, or religion,
we are brothers.

— Hypatia

Hatred does not cease by hatred at any time;
hatred ceases by love.

— Buddha

The meaning of life
is to live as if life and love were one.

— Ashley Montagu

The highest wisdom is kindness.

— Talmud

If you approach people with trust and affection,
you will have ten-fold trust and affection
returned to you.

— Mahatma Gandhi

With all beings and all things
we shall be as relatives.

— Black Elk

We wept so much that every one who passed by
Our tears, when he saw them flowing, said,
"What stream is this?"

— Hafez

The universe is but one great city,
full of beloved ones, divine and human,
by nature endeared to each other.

— Epictetus

Selfishly I give
love — for each grain I give, ten
thousand are returned.

— Hokkumeboshi

By the practice of loving kindness
I have attained liberation of heart.

— Buddha

The bird a nest, the spider a web, man friendship.

— William Blake

Do not remove a fly from your friend's forehead with a hatchet.

— Chinese saying

Love is never lost. If not reciprocated it will flow back and soften and purify the heart.

— Washington Irving

Love is eternal — the aspect may change, but not the essence. There is the same difference in a person before and after he is in love as there is in an unlighted lamp and one that is burning. The lamp was there and was a good lamp, but now it is shedding light too, and that is its real function. And love makes one calmer about many things, and that way, one is more fit for one's work.
— Vincent Van Gogh

The courteous learn their courtesy from the discourteous.

— Turkish saying

Of course anyone would have reassured a child, but something quite different seemed to have happened in that solitary meeting; and if I had been his own son, he could not have looked at me with eyes shining with greater love.

— Fyodor Dostoyevsky

Among Orientals, giving is a privilege.

— Elie Wiesel

Love cannot be forced, love cannot be coaxed and teased. It comes out of Heaven, unasked and unsought.

— Pearl Buck

Love is all we have
the only way that each
can help the other.

— Euripides

Doing good to others is not a duty. It is a joy, for it increases your own health and happiness.

— Zoroaster

No drop of love is ever wasted.

— Andre Gide

As he thought of his condition, it rather terrified and nauseated him. To think, after having known this one hour of wonder and superlative bliss, of being compelled to come back into the work-a-day world!

— Theodore Dreiser, *The Genius*

When we have learned to love not our separate life, but all living things, then at last we shall find peace.

— Buddha

CHILDREN

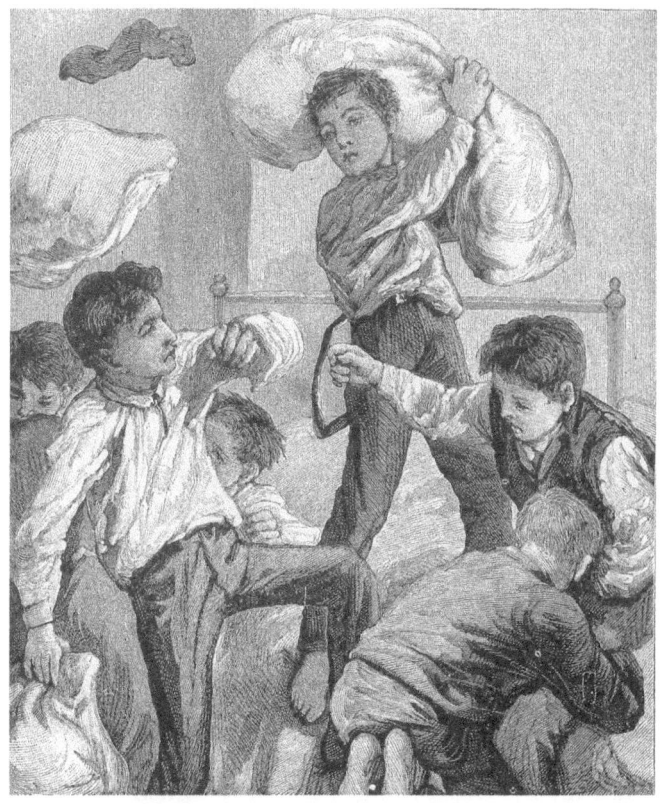

Before offering
sweets, or waving mean sticks — I
stop to see this child!

— *Hokkumeboshi*

The secret of genius is to carry the spirit of the child into old age, which means never losing your enthusiasm.

— Aldous Huxley

What a distressing contrast there is between the radiant intelligence of the child and the feeble mentality of the average adult.

— Sigmund Freud

Every child is an artist. The problem is how to remain an artist once he grows up.

— Pablo Picasso

Children need love, especially when they do not deserve it.

— H.S. Hulbert

Childhood is the world of miracle and wonder; as if creation rose, bathed in light, out of the darkness, utterly new and fresh and astonishing. The end of childhood is when things cease to astonish us. When the world seems familiar, when one has got used to existence, one has become an adult.

— Eugene Ionesco

I do not teach children, I give them joy.

— Isadora Duncan

The three most important rules for working with children are: Be sincere; Be sincere; and Be sincere.

— Michael Pastore

Children are remarkable for their intelligence and enthusiasm, for their curiosity, their intolerance of shams, the clarity and ruthlessness of their vision.

— Aldous Huxley

What does it mean that our children are better informed than ever before? That they know what the elders know. It means that they have become adults, or, at least, adult-like. It means — to use a metaphor of my own — that in having access to the previously hidden fruit of adult information, they are expelled from the garden of childhood.

— Neil Postman

If a child is to keep alive his inborn sense of wonder, he needs the companionship of at least one adult who can share it, rediscovering with him the joy, excitement and mystery of the world we live in.

— Rachel Carson

He threw himself upon his knees and Mary went down beside him. They had come upon a whole clump of crocuses burst into purple and orange and gold. Mary bent her face down and kissed them and kissed them.

— Frances Hodgson Burnett, *The Secret Garden*

You can only love a child
if you become a child yourself.

— A.S. Neill

The future of mankind depends on
the education of children.

— Aristotle

In old days there were angels who came and took men by the hand and led them away from the city of destruction. We see no white-winged angels now. But yet men are led away from threatening destruction: a hand is put into theirs, which leads them forth gently towards a calm and bright land, so that they look no more backward; and the hand may be a little child's.

— George Eliot

Too often we give children answers to remember
rather than problems to solve.

— Roger Lewin

In the beginning he used to shake his head
and wonder how it could be that the children
understood everything that I said and almost
nothing that he said; and then he laughed at me
when I told him that neither of us could teach the
children anything, but that they could teach us.

— Fyodor Dostoyevsky, *The Idiot*

If there is anything we wish to change in the child,
we should first examine it and see whether it is not
something that could better be changed in ourselves.

— Carl Gustav Jung

But a child only makes moral progress
when he is happy. The true maxim runs that
if we are happy we shall be good.

— Homer Lane

If a child tells a lie, tell him that he has told a lie, but
don't call him a liar. If you define him as a liar, you
break down his confidence in his own character.

— Jean Paul Richter

But punishment of children comes under the
heading of adult interference with life itself. Facing
the question frankly and openly we have to grant
that most punishing stems from the irritation of
adults simply because childhood is not young
adulthood; children and grown-ups are in many
ways antagonists in their interests.

— A. S. Neill

Children have never been very good at listening to
their elders, but they have never failed to imitate
them.

— James Baldwin

> The difficult child is the child who is unhappy. He is at war with himself; and in consequence he is at war with the whole world.
>
> — A.S. Neill

> The fault no child every loses is
> the one he is punished for.
>
> — Cesare Beccaria

A Russian Princess told Tolstoy's grandmother that (the Princess) believes it is necessary to act upon children through fear, and for that reason she beats the children.
 Tolstoy's grandmother replied:
 "That is very nice, only please, tell me, what refined feelings can you after that expect of your children?"

> — Leo Tolstoy

> Power is like holding an egg in your hand.
> If you hold too tightly, you crush the egg;
> if you hold too loosely,
> you drop the egg and it breaks.
>
> — African saying

> We can easily forgive a child who is afraid of the dark; the real tragedy of life is when men are afraid of the light.
>
> — Plato

The pupil is thereby "schooled" to confuse teaching with learning, grade advancement with education, a diploma with competence, and fluency with the ability to say something new.

— Ivan Illich

Cities are the abyss of the human species. At the end of a few generations the races perish or degenerate. They must be renewed, and it is always the country which provides for this renewal. Send your children, then, to renew themselves, as it were, to regain in the midst of the fields the vigor that is lost in the unhealthy air of overpopulated places.

— Jean-Jacques Rousseau

When children are doing nothing, they are doing mischief.

— Henry Fielding

It is too often required of children that they should adjust themselves to the world, practised and alert. But it would be more to the purpose that the world should adjust itself to children in all dealings with them.

— Alice Meynell

SACRED DUST

We are of dust
and short is the span of life.

— Howard Pyle, in *Robin Hood*

Life is a shadow and a mist;
it passes quickly by,
and is no more.

— African saying

One life:
a little gleam of time
between two eternities;
No second chance forevermore.

— *Thomas Carlyle*

All that happens to us is divinely great, and we are always in the center of a great world. But we must accustom ourselves to live like an angel who has just sprung to life, like a woman who loves, or like a man on the point of death.

If you knew that you were going to die tonight, or merely that you would have to go away and never return, would you, looking upon men and things for the last time, see them in the same light that you have hitherto seen them?

Or would you love as you never yet have loved?

— Maurice Maeterlinck

In a journey of a hundred miles,
the ninety-ninth mile
is to be considered the halfway point.

— Japanese saying

I follow nature as the surest guide, and surrender myself with faithful obedience to her sacred laws.

— Cicero

Paradise is wherever I am.

— Voltaire

Now I see the secret of making the best persons.
It is to grow in the open air
and to eat and sleep with the earth.

— Walt Whitman

Why do you not leave everything to the
great law of the universe and pass each
day with a peaceful smile?

— Zengetsu

Death? Life? Why bother
thinking about something that
happens only once?

— Hokkumeboshi

My candle laughs at
the wind: "The harder you blow,
the brighter I glow."

— Hokkumeboshi

Begin to live at once,
and count each day as a separate life.

— Seneca

Oh
snail,
Climb Mt. Fuji,
But slowly, slowly!

— Issa

Ride your horse along the edge of a sword;
Hide yourself in the middle of the flame.

— Zen saying

I live each moment as if it were my last!

— Alexis Zorba

Think twice before accepting honey
which is offered on a sharp knife.

— Tibetan saying

To be for one day entirely at leisure
is to be for one day an immortal.

— Chinese saying

A Deep-Sworn Vow

Others because you did not keep
That deep-sworn vow have been friends of mine;
Yet always when I look death in the face,
When I clamber to the heights of sleep,
Or when I grow excited with wine,
Suddenly I meet your face.

— William Butler Yeats

Will you agree that I have as much spirit of prophecy in me as the swans? For they, when they perceive that they must die, having sung all their life long, do then sing more lustily than ever, rejoicing in the thought that they are going to the god they serve.

— Socrates

Voice of my childhood
you call me ... Kwatz! I am too
far away to hear.

— Hokkumeboshi

The older we grow the more we realize that true power and happiness comes to us only from those who spiritually mean something to us. Whether they are near or far, still alive or dead, we need them if we are to find our way through life. The good we bear within us can be turned into life and action only when they are near to us in spirit.

— Albert Schweitzer

Acquit me or do not acquit me;
but be sure that I shall not alter
my way of life, no, not if I have
to die for it many times.

— Socrates

Work diligently
for your freedom from sorrow.

— Buddha, last words before dying

My heart is heavy; from the present
  It yearns towards those old days again,
When still the world seemed fair and pleasant,
  And men lived happy, free from pain.

Now all things seem at six and sevens,
  A scramble and a constant dread;
Dead is the Lord God in the heavens,
  Below us is the devil dead.

And all folks sad and mournful moving,
  Wear such a cross, cold, anxious face;
Were there not still a little loving,
  There would not be a resting place.

— Heinrich Heine

To You
who once lived
so kindly in this world
and now live in the heart
of each of us
you loved.

— Ming Li

Zenlightenment

I swear to you there are divine things
more beautiful than words can tell.

— *Walt Whitman*

Incipit vita nuova.
(The new life begins.)

— *Dante Alighieri*

If you bring forth what is within you,
what you bring forth
will save you.
If you do not bring forth what is within you,
what you do not bring forth
will destroy you.

— *Gnostic Gospels*

He who every morning plans the activities of the day, and then follows out that plan, carries a thread that will guide him through the labyrinth of the most busy life. The orderly arrangement of his time is like a ray of light which darts itself through all his occupations. But where no plan is laid, where the disposal of time is surrendered merely to the chance of incidents, chaos will soon reign.

— Victor Hugo

I have made a ceaseless effort not to ridicule, not to bewail, not to scorn human actions, but to understand them.

— Baruch Spinoza

Not in Utopia,— in subterranean fields, —
Or some secreted islands, Heaven knows where!
But in the very world, which is the world
Of all of us, — the place where, in the end,
We find our happiness, or not at all!

— William Wordsworth
(*Prelude*, BK II, lines 140-145)

To rejoice in life, to find the world beautiful and delightful to live in, was a mark of the Greek spirit which distinguished it from all that had gone before. It is a vital distinction.

— Edith Hamilton, in *The Greek Way*

Everything on the terrestrial globe has been weighed and measured, named and docketed, leaving in the physical realm nothing but the stars as objects for flights of fancy. More and more, therefore, must the spirit, impelled by the undying urge for knowledge, look inward, to probe its own enigmas. The internum aeternum, the spiritual universe, still offers art an inexhaustible domain. Man, as his knowledge widens, as he grows more fully conscious, will devote himself ever more boldly to the solution of an insoluble problem, to the discovery of his own soul, to the pursuit of self-knowledge.

— Stephan Zweig

One hour of life, crowded to the full with glorious action, and filled with noble risks, is worth whole years of those mean observances of paltry decorum.

— Walter Scott

To be a man is to be responsible. It is to feel shame at the sight of what seems to be unmerited misery.

— Antoine de Saint-Exupéry

I learned that every mortal will taste death.
But only some will taste life.

— Rumi

For there was never anyone yet
who could wholly escape love,
and never shall there be anyone,
never so long as beauty shall be,
never so long as eyes can see.

— Longus (*Daphnis and Chloe*)

Work is love made visible.

— Kahlil Gibran

Listening is the magic key that unlocks every heart. We must learn again how to listen, not with our ears only, but with the depths of our whole being — with our eyes, our warmth, our complete acceptance. Listening in this way, we give every person we meet a glowing gift she keeps and remembers for her whole life.
— Michael Pastore

It is incredible what a difference it makes to one's feelings toward the human race when one is treated with politeness in buses, trains, trams, subways, ferries, stores, ships, and streets.

— John Cowper Powys

There is no feeling in a human heart which exists in that heart alone — which is not, in some form or degree, in every heart.

— George MacDonald

Only connect! That was the whole of her sermon. Only connect the prose and the passion, and both will be exalted, and human love will be seen at its height. Live in fragments no longer. Only connect, and the beast and the monk, robbed of the isolation that is life to either, will die.

— E.M. Forster (*Howard's End*, 1910)

Light in the sky! Wake!
Again we walk this new road
My friend butterfly!

— Basho

A voice said to him, — why do you stay here and live this mean moiling life, when a glorious existence is possible for you?

— Henry David Thoreau

You have three days to live and two are gone.

— Sufi saying

The Wise Woman and the Dying Man

by Michael Pastore

In the middle of my life, my fortieth birthday on the first day of July, a terrible fever struck me down. My head burned; my muscles ached; my entire body felt lifeless and weak. With a great effort, I raised my eyelids, then rang the bell that called a servant to my side.

"Find a healer," I told him. "And to make certain that he is genuine, tell him that he is needed to ease the agony of a very poor man, who cannot pay in money but only in gratitude." My tearful servant bowed, then ran with all his energy to complete this urgent task.

Another servant rushed to my bedside awaiting my command. "Cancel all my appointments," I said, "for today and every day thereafter. Disinvite the guests from my birthday celebration this evening — tell them that I have departed on a journey, a journey perilous, inevitable and brief. Pack half my gold onto the back of a donkey, and then distribute it equally to the poor and needy in this town. The remaining gold give to the servants and workers who have served me faithfully during the years I slaved to make my fortune." When this servant, also in tears, departed on his errand, a third servant appeared with parchment paper and a peacock-feather quill pen, so I could write my last testament and will regarding my house, my possessions, and my precious books.

One hour later, as I gazed at the dark clouds, my first servant returned with the healer, who kneeled down at my bedside. Her body looked lithe and youthful; her posture, perfect; her hair white as a flower petal; her face beamed bright and cheerful as a happy child. She pressed her hands around my forehead, and then rubbed my face with rose-water.

"How long before I die?" I asked her.

"You have been terribly unhappy," she said. "The life of work and money that you are living on the outside has made you forget the life you might be living — a life of love and creativity — desired by your heart within. Your misery and forgetting has brought your body near to death."

"For healing and recovery," I asked, "is there no hope at all?"

The woman looked at me intensely, and then softly said: "There is one way, one way only, to save yourself. Beginning this moment you must change your life."

I shook my doubting head. "How can this impossible task be accomplished by a man so weak, so discouraged, and so consumed with despair at the world's evils and foolishness?"

With great concentration she studied my fiery eyes. "You have recently been to the town?" she asked.

"Yes, yesterday."

"What did you see there that looked extraordinary?"

"I saw nothing. Nothing at all."

She mixed a cold drink for me, made of yogurt, cucumbers, lemons, ginger, water and leaves of dill.

"Drink this," she said. "Now, put on your clothes and walking shoes. We must visit this town, the one place on earth where nothing extraordinary happens, and there are no life-lessons to be learned."

I shook my throbbing head. "I would rather stay here in this soft bed, and let my final moments be lightened by dancers shedding seven diaphanous veils. For traveling I am far too weak."

"Courage, man!" she shouted. "There is no choice, so you must be brave. If we do not attempt this journey, then you will never change. From your unhappiness your body will grow weaker and weaker and then you shall surely die."

Together, slowly, arm in arm, we walked six miles to the center of the town. We met an old man, his body bent from age like the letter gamma, shuffling forward no faster than a snail. I had seen him yesterday, and many times before, but I noticed nothing extraordinary about him.

"You work your life away," he said. Grasping his white-haired head, he glanced at his bent and aching body. "And now — this!"

My healer touched his shoulder.

"How would you live if you were young again?"

He answered without hesitating one instant. "If I could be young again, I would shout to every person in the world: 'Take care of your sacred body. There is nothing — nothing! — nothing more important than your body and your health.'"

Onward we walked, until the humming of an old woman captured our attention. I had seen her in the town, many times, but never noticed anything about her that might be interesting, unusual or unique.

"Tell us your story, old woman," said my bright-eyed companion, as she stroked the woman's hair.

"A man loved me once," she said. "But I lost him because I did not understand what love is. I did not appreciate the beauty of his unselfish love."

"How would you live if you were young again?" my healer asked.

"If I could be young again, I would love more deeply, I would devote myself to learning the mysterious art of love. Genuine love is not a mere feeling, it is actions: giving, caring, sharing, and sometimes, sacrifice."

I felt tired, yet we walked more into the center of the town where we met an artist, painting on a canvas in the park. My healer admired his work.

"This is nothing," he confessed. "I am a mediocre artist, yet I could have been a great artist."

"What would you do if you were young again?"

"If I were young again, I would work at my art two more hours every day, and I would master the secret of the greatest artists: how to concentrate intensely."

My lovely healer gave me a cup of water to drink, and then we walked until we found a child crying. His father had told him to quit playing and to go inside. When the child refused, the father threatened a punishment, but the child refused once more. Then the father, cheerfully, picked up his son and carried him to their house.

"Now," my healer told me, "we must return to your bedroom so that you can rest." Arriving there, she placed me on the bed, covered me with blankets, gave me drinks, rubbed my face and body with a warm oil, then took my hand and whispered, "Now, sleep."

That good sleep overflowed with strange and marvelous dreams. In one dream I saw my father and mother in their house, the house they had lost to debts and carelessness. They had returned to that house, unaware that it had been lost to creditors. I understood that the dream was not about my father but about the life I was living: How could I break the cycle of harmful actions, and live not imprisoned by the past? ... In another dream I saw myself working like a slave to build my business, and I realized that never had I bothered to ask: How can one acquire wealth without harming others, and without the ceaseless work that decimates a man's soul? ... In a third dream I saw that the town was in great danger from an approaching army, but the people seemed oblivious and unconcerned. Every evening, they gathered around the storytellers to listen to fantastic tales. In the dream I wondered aloud: How can we enjoy life without losing ourselves in the childish fantasies of these storytellers, who distract us from the deeper joys of being and loving and genuine creative work?

Shafts of light pierced my bedroom windows; birds twittered and squirrels chattered as they leaped across the branches. Slowly, I awakened. My body ached in ten places but the fever had vanished. I glanced up at the smiling face of my healer.

"I promised myself," said I, "that if I survived this illness, then I would live differently. And I promised that you, dear companion, would live here in my house and eat at my table for as long as it pleases you to stay."

Her warm hand touched my arm. "Do you remember what you heard and learned before your long rejuvenating sleep?"

After one blank minute I suddenly remembered. "Health is the first treasure; and then selfless love; and then the deep concentration of the great creators. ... I do not yet understand the meaning of the crying and rebellious child."

My companion smiled. "A lost fortune," she said, "can be made again; a demolished house can be rebuilt; a runaway camel can be found. But there is one dream in your heart that you must always remember. If you forget your dream, nothing can help you. If you carry your dream with you, you shall survive all your misfortunes and all your tears. "

I grasped her soft hands with my rough worker's hands. "And now, my wondrous healer," I said, "can you give me a gift so that I can never forget what I have almost died to learn?"

"There!" she said, pointing to the sky. "In the day, the blue sky and the clouds is your memento, and at night, the thousand thousand stars."

As she kissed my forehead, at last I understood an ancient jewel of wisdom. There is no salvation, there is no help from the outside. There is one way to save yourself and to save those persons and things you treasure. You must rely on yourself, on your own energy, ingenuity, and efforts.

Taking one deep breath, I stood up from the soft bed, ready to begin my new life. As I walked vigorously toward the garden, I heard my companion singing joyfully. At first, I could not make out the words, they seemed more like the song of a nightingale at the first red-gold glow of sunset. Suddenly, as I understood, great tears fell from my enlightened eyes.

The wise woman sang:

"Do not waste one hour, one minute, one moment of your life. Love tenderly. Love passionately. Love with your whole heart on fire. Live every moment giving love."

Index — Feast of Authors

Abelard, Peter (1079–1142) 90
African saying 19, 29, 54, 64, 71, 114, 142, 145
Andersen, Hans Christian (1805–1875) 73
Aristophanes (448 B.C.E.– 385 B.C.E.) 60
Aristotle (384–322 B.C.E.) 56, 79, 98, 140
Armenian saying 56
Arnold, Matthew (1822–1888) 37, 119
Aurelius, Marcus (121–180) 4, 43
Austen, Jane (1775–1817) 58

Baldwin, James (1924–1987) 141
Balzac, Honore de (1799–1850) 55
Basho, Matsuo (1644–1694) 155
Beccaria, Cesare (1738–1794) 142
Bhagavad Gita (ca. 350 B.C.E.– 300 C.E.) 21, 113
Black Elk (1863–1950) 102, 104, 132
Blake, William (1757–1827) 27, 29, 69, 104, 113, 128, 133
Blyth, R(obert) H(enderson) (1919–1970) 118
Boccaccio, Giovanni (1313–1375) 86
Brontë, Emily (1818–1848) 37
Brooks, Van Wyck (1886–1963) 49
Buber, Martin (1878–1965) 9, 110, 124 (same as p.9)
Buck, Pearl (1892–1973) 135
Buddha [Gautama Siddartha] (563–483 B.C.E.) 16, 75, 93, 106, 112, 115, 124, 129, 131, 133, 136, 149
Buffon, Georges Louis Leclerc de (1707–1788) 82
Bulgarian saying 65
Burmese saying 113
Burnett, Frances Hodgson (1849–1924) 139
Burroughs, John (1837–1921) 80
Buson, Yosa (1716–1784) 124

Cage, John (1912–1992) 58
Carlyle, Thomas (1795–1881) 16, 145
Carson, Rachel (1907–1964) 139

Cary, Joyce (1888–1957) 28
Casanova, Giacomo (1725–1798) 127
Cavafy, C. P. (1863–1933) 84
Cervantes, Miguel de (1547–1616) 131
Chaplin, Charlie (1889–1977) 88
Chapman, John Jay (1862–1933) 129
Chesterton, G(ilbert) K(eith) (1874-1936) 39
Chinese saying 29, 56, 64, 65, 70, 71, 72, 76, 80, 134, 149
Churchill, Winston (1874–1965) 73
Cicero, Marcus Tullius (106–43 B.C.E.) 146
Confucius [K'ung Fu-Tzu] (551–479 B.C.E.) 49, 68, 83, 94, 95, 96, 101, 118
Cummings, Edward Estlin (1894–1962) 70
Czech saying 46

Daibi of Unkan (1882–1964) 118
Dante Alighieri (1265–1321) 151
Defoe, Daniel (1659–1731) 39
Dhammapada (ca. 30 B.C.E.) 22, 32, 69, 79
Dickens, Charles (1812–1870) 123
Dickinson, Emily (1830–1886) 40
Diderot, Denis (1713–1784) 57
Disraeli, Benjamin (1804–1881) 69, 81
Dostoyevsky, Fyodor (1821–1881) 65, 68, 69, 128, 135, 140
Doyle, Arthur Conan (1859–1930) 23
Dreiser, Theodore (1871–1945) 67, 135
Duncan, Isadora (1878–1927) 138
Durant, Will (1885–1981) 96

Eckhart, Meister (1260–1328) 26
Einstein, Albert (1879–1955) 66
Ekken, Kaibara (1630–1714) 44
Eliot, George (1819–1880) 34, 140
Ellis, Havelock (1859–1939) 120
Emerson, Ralph Waldo (1803–1882) 23, 25, 26, 54, 76, 77, 78, 87, 96, 108, 116, 117
English tongue twister 44
Epictetus (ca. 50 – ca.138) 33, 43, 133

Euripides (484–406 B.C.E.) 32, 135

Fielding, Henry (1707–1754) 143
Flaubert, Gustave (1821–1880) 56
Fleming, Ian (1908–1964) 87
Forster, E. M. (1879–1970) 85, 155
France, Anatole (1844-1924) 79, 87
Franklin, Benjamin (1706–1790) 18
Fromm, Erich (1900–1980) 20, 63
Freud, Sigmund (1856–1939) 138

Gabirol, Solomon Ibn (1021–1058) 62
Gandhi, Mohandas Karamchand (1869–1948) 92, 93, 96, 101, 105, 131, 132
Gibran, Kahlil (1883–1931) 154
Gide, Andre (1869–1951) 114, 135
Giono, Jean (1895–1970) 94
Gnostic Gospels (third century, C.E.) 151
Goethe, Johann Wolfgang von (1749–1832) 18, 53, 76, 82, 89, 127
Goldsmith, Oliver (1730–1774) 48, 76
Goncharov, Ivan (1812–1891) 85
Gorky, Maxim [Aleksei Peshkov] (1868–1936) 71, 84
Gracian, Baltasar (1601–1658) 83
Greek sailor 35

Hafez (1325–1390) 133
Hamilton, Edith (1867–1963) 152
Hasidic saying 32, 44, 64, 78
Hawthorne, Nathaniel (1804–1864) 66
Heine, Heinrich (1797–1856) 87, 150
Heraclitus (576–480 B.C.E.) 116
Hesse, Hermann (1877–1962) 105
Hindu saying 80, 112
Hoffmann, E.T.A. (1776–1822) 57
Hokkumeboshi (1900–) 4, 8, 13, 14, 19, 21, 24, 31, 42, 43, 45, 50, 51, 53, 57, 61, 63, 64, 68, 69, 70, 71, 73, 74, 83, 88, 100, 102, 109, 111, 114, 124, 133, 137, 147, 148

Hokusai, Katsushika (1760–1849) 72, 79
Homer (8th century B.C.E.) 22
Horace (65–8 B.C.E.) 33
Howe, Eric Graham (1897– 1971) 112
Hudson, William Henry (1841–1922) 42
Hugo, Victor (1802–1885) 152
Hulbert, Harold S. (1887 – 1949) 138
Huxley, Aldous (1894–1963) 33, 138, 139
Huxley, Thomas Henry (1825–1895) 19
Hypatia (350?–415?) 131

I Ching 59
Ibsen, Henrik (1828–1906) 95
Illich, Ivan (1926–2002) 143
Indian proverb 70
Ionesco, Eugene (1909–1994) 138
Irish saying 71
Irving, Washington (1783–1859) 134
Issa, Kobayashi (1763–1828) 147

Jacobsen, Jens Peter (1847–1885) 59
James, William (1842–1910) 88
Japanese saying 113, 146
Jesus of Nazareth (4 B.C.E.–29 C.E.) 92
Johnson, Samuel (1709–1784) 88
Jung, Carl Gustav (1875–1961) 141

Kazantzakis, Nikos (1885–1957) 13, 35, 83, 110, 112, 119
Kierkegaard, Soren Aabye (1813–1855) 76
Kyozan Ejaku (771– 853) 57

La Bruyere, Jean de (1645–1696) 42
La Fontaine, Jean de (1621–1695) 15
Lagerlöf, Selma (1858–1940) 128
Lane, Homer (1875–1925) 141
Lao Tzu (604–517 B.C.E.) 93, 94, 95, 110, 131
Lawrence, D. H. (1885–1930) 59
Leonardo da Vinci (1452–1519) 54
Lewin, Roger (1944 –) 140

Lincoln, Abraham (1809–1865) 23, 62
London, Jack (1876–1916) 120–121
Longus (2nd century A.D.) 154

MacDonald, George (1824–1905) 155
Maeterlinck, Maurice (1862–1949) 53, 146
Marx, Karl (1818–1883) 22
Masahide, Hirate (1492–1553) 38
Maskaleris, Thanasis (1930, Oct. 26–   ) 13–14, 84
Maugham, William Somerset (1874–1965) 35
Melville, Herman (1819–1891) 97
Mencius (372–289 B.C.E.) 92, 130
Meynell, Alice (1847–1922) 143
Michelangelo Buonarrotti (1475–1564) 56, 97
Miller, Henry (1891–1980) 82, 91
Milton, John (1608–1674) 116
Ming Li (? – ?) 17, 35, 36, 45, 46, 52, 53, 65, 71, 78, 80, 82, 90, 100, 103, 104, 105, 115, 116, 127, 150
Montagu, Ashley (1905–1999) 132
Montaigne, Michel de (1533–1592) 42, 110
More, Thomas (1478–1535) 73
Morris, William (1834–1896) 77
Mumford, Lewis (1895–1990) 98
Mussorgsky, Modest Petrovich (1835–1881) 52

Napoleon Bonaparte (1769–1821) 17
Neill, A. S. (1883–1973) 140, 141, 142
Nietzsche, Friedrich Wilhelm (1844–1900) 20, 37, 44, 77, 99, 115
Nigerian saying/song 34, 46

Ohsawa, Georges (1893–1966) 111
Oppenheim, E. Phillips (1866–1946) 47
Orczy, (Baroness) Emma (1865–1947) 38
Ortega & Gasset, José (1883–1955) 117
Ovid (43 B.C.E–C.E. 18) 104

Papillon [Henri Charriere] (1906–1973) 20
Pastore, Michael (too late—too soon) 6, 18, 21, 23, 38, 43, 47, 52, 58, 60, 63, 81, 82, 86, 102, 122, 126, 139, 154
Picasso, Pablo (1881–1973) 138
Plato (427–347 B.C.E.) 77, 142
Plutarch (46?–120) 33, 34
Po Chu-I (772–846) 36, 70
Postman, Neil (1931–2003) 139
Powys, John Cowper (1872–1963) 72, 154
Proust, Marcel (1871–1922) 58
Pyle, Howard (1853–1911) 48, 145
Pythagoras of Samos (570–495 B.C.E) 107

Rabelais, Francois (1494–1553) 45
Read, Herbert (1893–1968) 29
Red Jacket [Sa-Go-Ye-Wat-Ha] (1751?–1830) 103
Richter, Jean Paul (1763–1825) 141
Rilke, Rainer Maria (1875–1926) 52, 117
Rolland, Romain (1866–1944) 98
Rostand, Edmund (1868–1918) 94
Rousseau, Jean-Jacques (1712–1778) 143
Rumi, Jalal ad-Din Muhammad (1207–1273) 3, 39, 153
Ruskin, John (1819–1900) 27
Russell, Bertrand (1872–1970) 68
Russian saying 16, 68

Saint-Exupéry, Antoine de (1900–1944) 153
Sand, George (1804–1876) 130
Sappho (630 B.C.E–570 B.C.E.) 88
Saroyan, William (1908–1981) 120
Schopenhauer, Arthur (1788–1860) 28
Schweitzer, Albert (1875–1965) 64, 65, 149
Scott, Walter (1771–1832) 153
Seneca (8 B.C.E. – 65 C.E.) 17, 65, 79, 147
Sengai Gibon (1750–1837) 40, 100
Shakespeare, William (1564–1616) 90
Shaw, George Bernard (1856–1950) 16, 36, 54, 56
Shelley, Mary (1797–1851) 83
Shelley, Percy Bysshe (1792–1822) 49

Singer, Isaac Bashevis (1902–1991) 119
Socrates (470–399 B.C.E.) 34, 62, 91, 93, 108, 148, 149
Sozan, (Master) Genkyo (1797–1868) 83
Spanish proverb 84
Spinoza, Baruch (1632–1677) 80, 152
Steinbeck, John (1902–1968) 22
Stendhal [Marie Henri Beyle] (1783–1842) 127
Stephens, James (1882–1950) 86, 107
Sterne, Laurence (1713–1768) 70
Stowe, Harriet Beecher (1811–1896) 37
Sufi saying 106, 156
Symons, Arthur William (1865–1945) 53

Tagore, Rabindranath (1861–1941) 72
Talmud (ca. 500 C.E.) 46, 132
Tamil saying 27
T'ang Meng–lai (1627–1698) 26
Thales (640–546 B.C.E.) 66, 105
Thoreau, Henry David (1817–1862) 4, 30, 41, 47, 49, 53, 58, 62, 63, 72, 78, 80, 101, 108, 130, 155
Thoreau, O. (1980–   ) 47, 66
Tibetan saying 148
Tobias, Michael Charles (1952–   ) 91
Tolstoy, Leo (1828–1910) 19, 27, 142
Turkish saying 74, 134
Twain, Mark [Samuel Clemens] (1835–1910) 77

Ueland, Brenda (1891–1985) 95
Upanishads (began ca. 900 B.C.E.) 114, 115

van Gogh, Vincent (1853–1890) 17, 106, 134
Voltaire [Francois Marie Arouet] (1694–1778) 32, 77, 79, 90, 146

Walpole, Horace (1717–1797) 56
Whitman, Walt (1819–1892) 26, 81, 111, 117, 125, 146, 151
Wiesel, Elie (1928–   ) 135
Wilde, Oscar (1854–1900) 76, 124

Wilson, Colin (1931–2013) 28
Wolfe, Thomas (1900–1938) 66
Wordsworth, William (1770–1850) 152
Woolf, Virginia (1882–1941) 54
Wu-Ti (140–87 B.C.E.) 74

Xenophon (427 B.C.E.– 355 B.C.E.) 91

Yeats, William Butler (1865–1939) 60, 148
Yezierska, Anzia (1880–1970) 118
Yiddish saying 18, 20, 21, 57, 58, 102
Yosano Akiko (1878–1942) 69

Zengetsu (833–912) 147
Zimbabwe proverb 72
Zorba, Alexis (1876 ?–1946 ?) 148
Zoroaster (628–551 B.C.E.) 92, 136
Zweig, Stephan (1881–1942) 153
Zen saying 119, 147
Zengzi (505–435 B.C.E.) 82

About Zorba Press

Zorba Press is an independent publisher of books, ebooks, audio books, and films on DVDs. From the gorgeous gorges of Ithaca, New York, we publish the paperback books *The Zorba Anthology of Love Stories; The Ithaca Manual of Style;* and a wild novel about love and eros — *Thoreau Bound: A Utopian Romance in the Isles of Greece.*

Our most recent publications are *Sappho At The Edge Of Love: 100 Poems by Michael Pastore* (paperback and ebook and audiobook); *Kazantzakis: A Film By Michael Tobias* (video on DVD); *The Adventures of Mr Marigold* (ebook); the paperback and ebook editions of *My Life On The Ragged Paths Of Pan: Selected Poems and Translations of Thanasis Maskaleris;* and an anthology of wise and illuminating quotations called *Zenlightenment.*

At Zorba Press, we practice what we call "Sustainable Publishing": publishing with a greater sense of awareness and responsibility. Sustainable Publishing is the attempt to bring to the work of publishing a healthy balance between four essential elements: Culture, Commerce, Technology (humanized), and Nature.

Zorba's mission is to promote the innovative ideas and the daring books that nourish children and childhood, point the way to a culture of non-violence, create a sustainable future, and nurture — for every living being — a new world of love, kindness, courage, creativity, sincerity, peace, and happiness.

www.ingramcontent.com/pod-product-compliance
Lightning Source LLC
Chambersburg PA
CBHW020933090426
42736CB00010B/1124